SURVIVED BY ONE

The Elmer H. Johnson and Carol Holmes Johnson Series in Criminology

The Elmer H. Johnson and Carol Holmes Johnson Series in Criminology

SURVIVED BY ONE

The Life and Mind of
a Family Mass Murderer

Robert E. Hanlon
With Thomas V. Odle

Southern Illinois University Press
Carbondale

16 15 14 13   4 3 2 1

Publication of this book has been underwritten by The
Elmer H. Johnson and Carol Holmes Johnson Series in
Criminology fund.

Library of Congress Cataloging-in-Publication Data

Hanlon, Robert E., 1957–
Survived by one : the life and mind of a family mass
murderer / Robert E. Hanlon with Thomas V. Odle.
    pages cm. — (The Elmer H. Johnson and Carol Holmes
Johnson series in criminology)
Includes bibliographical references and index.
    ISBN-13: 978-0-8093-3262-5 (cloth : alk. paper)
    ISBN-10: 0-8093-3262-0 (cloth : alk. paper)
    ISBN-13: 978-0-8093-3263-2 (ebook)
    ISBN-10: 0-8093-3263-9 (ebook)
1. Odle, Thomas V. 2. Murderers—Illinois—Biography.
3. Mass murder—Illinois—Case studies. 4. Antisocial
personality disorders—Case studies. I. Title.
HV6248.O35H36 2013
364.152'34092—dc23
[B]   2012048886

Printed on recycled paper. ♻
The paper used in this publication meets the mini-
mum requirements of American National Standard for
Information Sciences—Permanence of Paper for Printed
Library Materials, ANSI Z39.48-1992. ∞

Contents

Gallery of illustrations follows page 78

Preface

On November 8, 1985, five members of the Odle family were brutally murdered in their home in a small town in Southern Illinois. Examination of the crime scene and autopsies revealed that four family members, including both parents and two children, had been repeatedly stabbed in the neck with a butcher knife. One child had been strangled to death. Forensic analysis revealed that the slayings were committed in a methodical manner over a period of eight hours. Tom Odle, the eldest son and only surviving member of the family, was charged with the murders the following day.

Tom Odle's trial revealed that his mother, Carolyn Odle, dominated the household. Although she was considered an upstanding member of the community and was president of the Parent-Teacher Organization (PTO) at her children's elementary school, the trial exposed her darker side, characterized by sadistic physical and mental abuse. Tom was ultimately convicted of five counts of first-degree murder and sentenced to death. He spent the next seventeen years on death row. On January 11, 2003, in response to the growing number of death-row prisoners who had been exonerated due to wrongful convictions, Illinois Governor George Ryan commuted the death sentences of all death-row inmates in Illinois, and Tom is now serving natural life.

Tom's life unfolds in three distinct acts. Act 1 covers the lifetime of physical and mental abuse that culminated in the five murders. Act 2 is his trial, sentencing, and seventeen years on death row. Act 3 begins the day his death sentence was commuted and he realized that he was not going to die, as he had thought for years. That realization led to a process of self-reflection and examination, a time during which he began to make something positive of his life. Tom reached out to me with questions regarding his mother, his personality, and his brain, as well as the key question: "Why'd I do it?" As a neuropsychologist, I had examined him years earlier. Under my direction, he engaged in a psychotherapeutic process during that introspective time, which involved writing about his life and the murders. That process of self-exploration and analysis led to the writing of this book.

Told in chronological order, *Survived by One: The Life and Mind of a Family Mass Murderer* is the story of a defiant and rebellious boy of superior intelligence and progresses from his earliest memories through years of physical and mental abuse by his mother. Drug abuse and petty

viii Preface

crime contribute to the events and dynamics that precipitated the brutal murder of all other members of his family, including his parents, Robert and Carolyn, and his three siblings, Robyn, fourteen, Sean, thirteen, and Scott, ten. The story progresses through his trial, conviction, and death sentence, including the results of psychological evaluations and psychiatric examinations by forensic experts and the testimony of friends, neighbors, and local educators.

After being sentenced to death at the age of nineteen, Tom was confronted with the hard, cold reality of life on death row. As he waited for his date with a needle, he watched other men leave the row to be executed. However, for each condemned man executed in Illinois during that time, another death-row inmate was exonerated and freed. This was the result of evidence presented on appeals that revealed an alarming trend of wrongful convictions in capital cases, due to false confessions obtained by police torture, perjury by key witnesses, prosecutorial misconduct, and corruption in the Illinois criminal-justice system. Seemingly oblivious to this trend, Tom occupied his time by reading, writing, and painting while patiently waiting to die.

I met Tom Odle when he was on death row. I was retained by his attorneys, Richard "Dick" Cunningham and Aviva Futorian, in November 1999. In January 2000, the governor of Illinois instituted a moratorium on executions in response to the fact that thirteen other death-row inmates in Illinois had been exonerated during a period of twelve years. At the request of Tom's attorneys, I conducted a neuropsychological evaluation of Tom on death row in January 2001 at the Pontiac Correctional Center of the Illinois Department of Corrections. The evaluation revealed that he possesses an IQ in the superior range of intelligence and that his cognitive functions and mental abilities are generally intact. Assessment of his personality revealed that he manifests personality traits consistent with antisocial personality disorder.

During the next three years, I had no contact with Tom. In 2003 came the commutation of death-row sentences.

Following Tom's sentence being changed to natural life without parole, I received a letter from him in which he said he was interested in trying to understand why he committed such a horrible crime and in learning more about antisocial personality disorder. I wrote back and provided him with some information about antisocial personality disorder and the psychological effects of long-term incarceration. This exchange resulted in more letters from Tom, who was clearly interested in gaining insight regarding his personality, his family, and his previous choices. As a result, I offered to assist him by engaging him in a therapeutic exercise of self-exploration and self-assessment via a series of letters. I offered to provide him with questions and outlines of topics if he would be willing to write, in detail, about his development, his family, his relationships with his mother and father, his juvenile crimes and drug abuse, and his thoughts and feelings preceding and during the murder of his family.

In response, I began receiving lengthy, single-spaced, two-sided, typed letters with detailed descriptions of his childhood experiences, his relationship with mother and father, his physical and emotional abuse, his drug abuse, his juvenile crimes, and the events that precipitated the murder of his family. However, during this time, he lost his typewriter due to a correctional policy and shifted to handwritten letters. I was impressed with his willingness for self-disclosure and his growing insight. Eventually, I visited him after he was transferred to the Lawrence Correctional Center in Sumner, Illinois, and we discussed the process, his progress, and his goals. He wondered if others might benefit from his story. At that point, we discussed the notion of publishing his story and subsequently initiated work on the manuscript. Excerpts from his letters are set off distinctively throughout the book. The names of some of his friends and acquaintances have been changed out of respect for their privacy. The names of individuals who formally gave permission to include their names and statements are cited. Similarly, the names of individuals whose names and statements are documented in the public record (e.g., court dockets, trial transcripts) or in previous publications (e.g., newspaper articles) are cited. Tom Odle receives no financial compensation for his contribution to this book

The only reason Tom Odle is alive today is because thirteen men were wrongfully convicted of murders they didn't commit and sentenced to death. If the moratorium had not been instituted, Tom Odle would have been executed, and, ironically, the redemptive element of his story would have been lost forever.

Acknowledgments

The author thanks the following individuals and institutions for their support and influence regarding this book: Aviva Futorian, for her continual support, legal instruction, and approval of this project; Kathleen Finley, for her emotional support, encouragement, and key suggestions regarding the creation of this book; Karl Kageff, editor-in-chief, Southern Illinois University Press, for his editorial suggestions and guidance in the publication process; Dr. David Adams; Judge Lori Wolfson; Dr. Lawrence Jeckel; Dr. Henry Conroe; Teri Clark, Illinois School District 80; former faculty members of Horace Mann School, Mt. Vernon, Illinois; faculty members of Mt. Vernon Township High School, Mt. Vernon, Illinois; Harry Karabel; the *Southern Illinoisan*; the *Morning Sentinel*; the *Mt. Vernon Register-News*; C. E. Brehm Memorial Public Library of Mt. Vernon, Illinois; Office of the State Appellate Defender; Center on Wrongful Convictions–Northwestern University Law School; Sandra Downey; Dr. James Knoll; Dimitri Beres; and the Illinois Department of Corrections.

SURVIVED BY ONE

Introduction

The Odle Family Mass Murder: A Rare Case of Parricidal Familicide

The deliberate, calculated, serial execution of all family members by one of the children is an extremely rare crime that represents less than 1 percent of all homicides in the world. *Survived by One* is the true story of one such unconscionable act.

The mass murder of the Odle family is one of the most horrific acts of parricidal familicide in U.S. history. The collective human response to a teenager murdering his entire family is, "How does something like this happen?" When the murderer himself, after years of incarceration and self-reflection, asks the same question, we are compelled to join him on a journey deep into the circumstances and dynamics that may explain, but not defend, this unforgivable act. Written in part by the killer himself, this book offers a firsthand account of the thoughts and experiences that led to his horrific crime. In a truly unique collaboration, this convicted mass murderer, Tom Odle, and I tell this tragic story of abuse, abandonment, annihilation, and atonement.

Understanding the Crime: Parricide and Familicide

In order to fully understand the gravity and unique nature of these crimes, a few definitions and statistics are in order.

There are multiple definitions of the term *familicide.* Neil Websdale, principle project adviser to and former director of the National Domestic Violence Fatality Review Initiative, defines *familicide* as "the deliberate killing within a relatively short period of time of a current or former spouse or intimate partner and one or more of their children, perhaps followed by the suicide of the perpetrator" (2010). Similarly, Wilson, Daly, and Daniele (1995) define *familicide* as the killing of a current or former spouse or intimate partner and one or more of their children. Grant Duwe (2004) refers to *familicide* as the killing of four or more family members by another family member within a twenty-four-hour period. The mass murder of the Odle family does not meet the criteria for *familicide* as outlined by Websdale (2010) and Wilson, Daly, and Daniele (1995), due to the fact that the murders were committed by one of the children rather than a parent. However, the Odle family murders clearly meet the criteria for *familicide* proposed by Duwe (2004).

Despite the differences in the definitions above, the fundamental feature that constitutes familicide is a family member killing multiple family members. Arguably one of the most disturbing types of domestic homicide, acts of familicide are usually committed by males, typically the husband and father. In most cases of familicide, the husband-father serially executes his wife and one or more of the children and commits suicide. The motives for such horrific crimes include the following: acts of desperation driven by severe mental illness, such as psychotic depression or delusions associated with other psychotic disorders; impulsive acts committed by chronically depressed men plagued with long-standing feelings of inferiority, insecurity, and inadequacy, with a concomitant drug or alcohol addiction, who are intoxicated at the time of the killings; premeditated and planned executions committed by narcissistic antisocial men with psychopathic tendencies intended to quickly and efficiently dispose of the family in order to enable them to freely pursue other love interests or sexual endeavors.

The term *parricide* refers to the killing of a parent by a child and includes acts of *matricide* (killing of a mother or stepmother) and *patricide* (killing of a father or stepfather). Although relatively rare, such murders commonly elicit considerable attention from the media. Criminologist Kathleen Heide, among others, has conducted extensive research on the topic of parricide (1989, 1992, 1995). In an extensive search of international electronic databases, Boots and Heide (2006) found that a total of 226 cases of parricide, worldwide, had been reported by the media since 1870, with 208 of those cases reported between 1980 and 2003. Of these 226 cases, 150 occurred in the United States. In 85 percent of these cases, sons killed one or both parents. Of the cases in which conviction data were available, 26 percent resulted in a conviction of first-degree murder.

Of those convicted of first-degree murder, 8 offenders were sentenced to death. Tom Odle is one of the 8 individuals known to have been sentenced to death for parricide between 1870 and 2003.

Although severe forms of mental illness, such as paranoid schizophrenia, bipolar disorder, and other psychotic disorders, have been implicated in acts of parricide, child abuse is the most common factor cited in motivational analyses of parricidal acts (e.g., Ewing, 2001; Heide, 1992, 1995, 1999). In reaction to the growing awareness of the high prevalence of a history of abuse of the offender by the victim in cases of parricide, Heide (1992) proposes a model that classifies parricide offenders into one of three types, based on primary motive: (1) children who have suffered chronic physical, sexual, and/or mental abuse kill their parents to end the abuse; (2) children who manifest a severe mental disorder kill their parents in relation to psychotic symptoms, such as paranoid delusions or command hallucinations; and (3) dangerously antisocial children who kill their parents for personal gain, such as inheritance or freedom from parental control.

Parricidal familicide refers to the killing of one or both parents and one or more siblings by a child (Leggett, 2000). Although extremely rare, most reported cases of parricidal familicide involve the mass murder of all other family members, including both parents and all siblings, by the eldest male child. Criminologist Virginia Leggett conducted an exhaustive search for documented incidents of parricidal familicide in Texas from 1978 to 1998. During this twenty-year period, over forty-three thousand murders were committed in Texas, but only four incidents of parricidal familicide occurred. Upon reviewing the details of these four crimes, including hypothetical motives and aspects of the relationships between offenders and victims, she concludes that acts of parricidal familicide are driven by the offender's resentment of his lack of autonomy and of dependence on the family. The offender, according to Leggett, comes to believe that he must kill his family to restore his own life and free himself from the control of the family unit. Similarly, anthropologist Elliott Leyton, author of *Sole Survivor: Children Who Murder Their Families* (1990), proposes that the offender in cases of parricidal familicide, who is often the victim of long-term abuse by one or both parents, kills the family to escape an oppressive and/or abusive situation in which he feels entrapped.

1

Mother and Son

The city of Mt. Vernon, Illinois, was established in 1817 and named after George Washington's home and plantation on the Potomac River. Town founder Zadok Casey was a career politician who was elected to the state senate in 1822, became lieutenant governor in 1833, and served in the U.S. Congress between 1833 and 1843 (Mt. Vernon, Illinois, 2011). It is easy to imagine his Washingtonian aspirations for this spot at the crossroads of Southern Illinois. But the town's character, fueled by economic and historical trends as well as a natural disaster, would grow in a different direction.

On February 19, 1888, a tornado swept across the broad, flat Illinois plains, cutting a path a half mile wide through Mt. Vernon, killing 37 people and destroying the Jefferson County Courthouse and more than 450 houses. In one of its first efforts as an organization, the American Red Cross responded to the disaster. Its founder, heroine Clara Barton, directed the relief efforts (City of Mt. Vernon, 2011; Wikipedia, 2011j).

As an outgrowth of the relief efforts, the Mt. Vernon Car Manufacturing Company opened in 1889. The Louisville and Nashville Railroad delivered over nineteen hundred carloads of supplies for the town's reconstruction. This increased rail traffic led to Mt. Vernon's big industry: building railroad cars. By 1909, the "car shops" produced twenty-five cars per day, employed more than a thousand workers, and had a $60,000 a month payroll (City of Mt. Vernon, 2011; Wikipedia, 2011j). Mt. Vernon would rarely stray from its hardworking, blue-collar roots.

In the 1960s, Mt. Vernon was a town of many working-class neighborhoods, small, tidy houses with detached garages, the residences separated from each other by carports and chain-link fences. Because the city's population never exceeded twenty thousand, people knew each other. Neighbors talked across the fence, waved hello as they passed, stopped to chat in the grocery stores. Hot, drowsy summers gave way to quick, crisp winters that brought the occasional light dusting of snow and, almost inevitably, an early spring. Into one of these working-class families, Tom Odle was born.

First Memories and Early Childhood

My earliest memories are from when I was about 4 or 5 years old, and they are about my parents. One memory, in particular, was when I was about four years old. When I was little, I always had to play by myself. I wasn't allowed in the living room very often because my mother didn't want to be around me, I guess. At that time, my room was next to the living room. I was playing a bit too loud, and my mother came in and slammed my head into the wall several times. I specifically recall this incident because it was the only time that my mother ever came back into my room, after hitting me, to apologize for flying off the handle. But I recall this incident more because it was the only time I ever remember her telling me that she loved me. Those words made every-thing okay, again, and I felt loved by her.

Another memory from about the same time involved an incident when my paternal grandparents were at our house. We were all in the backyard. Everyone was sitting around in lawn chairs, except me and my dad. We were playing catch with a baseball. I threw the ball to my dad. It was a little wild, and it broke a window. Nobody got upset, except my mother, who spanked me in front of everyone and then made me go sit on my bed. My dad and my grandma and grandpa came in the room and asked me if I was okay. But my mom never came in. It was an accident, but my mom swore I did it on purpose.

I remember going to my grandparents' house a lot and helping my grandpa work in the garden. I also remember going for rides in the car on Sunday with my grandma and grandpa. I always loved to go to my grandparents' house because I was away from home. I always felt welcome in my grandparents' house, unlike at home. I just never felt like I belonged there, even when I was little. And, I could never shake that feeling the rest of my life. I remember one time we were going to the store when my mother was pregnant with my sister. We were running and she tripped and fell. She cut her chin and had to get some stitches. She called my father at work and he came home. Then she told him that I tripped her, on purpose. But it was an accident and I never touched her. I couldn't understand why she said such a thing. And, the look I got from my dad was one I'll never forget because that was the first time I felt like he did not like me anymore. I never shook that look from my mind.

Carolyn Odle and Physical Abuse

November 8, 1985, was a day unlike any other in the lives of Bob and Carolyn Odle and their family. And it was a day that the residents of the small town of Mt. Vernon, Illinois, will never forget. Autumn lingered, but the first signs of the approaching winter had appeared. The sky was overcast, and the air held a chill that warned of an early frost. Soon the wind and snow would sweep across the frozen farmlands surrounding the little town. But the chill that hung over the Odle home that day was influenced less by the temperature than by the ominous specter of unimaginable horror that was to come.

Carolyn's activities that day were typical for a busy housewife, homemaker, and mother of four who tried her best to stay involved in community activities. She had bowled the night before, and as treasurer of the local bowling league, she needed to stop at the bank to deposit money collected from league members. She also volunteered in the school library. She had recently accepted an appointment as president of the Parent Teacher Organization (PTO) at Horace Mann Elementary School, the school all of her children had attended. In fact, that morning she had scheduled a meeting of the planning committee for the annual chili dinner in the school library. Afterwards, she had to get home by 11:30 A.M. to fix her husband's lunch.

Seven months later, during her son's murder trial, mental-health professionals and forensic experts would describe this seemingly typical homemaker, mother of four, and PTO president as "sadistic" and "abusive." The malignant disparity between the image of the PTO president and the sadistically abusive mother was a source of both contention and wonder. The Odle family photo, which appeared on the front page of local newspapers shortly after the murders, depicted what appeared to be an average, middle-class American family. But the court would learn that despite the persona of loving mother and school volunteer the photo and her public actions suggested, Carolyn was a controlling, manipulative, and emotionally detached woman with a penchant for corporal punishment. The court would also learn that Tom Odle's core motive for the mass murder of the entire Odle family was to kill Carolyn. As in most cases of parricide, the correlation between the public persona and the private life of the maternal target is complex. For the court and the people of Mt. Vernon, Illinois, the correlation between Carolyn Louise Odle, PTO president, and the allegedly abusive woman brutally murdered by her son was unfathomable.

> My mother was a very strict woman. I was never allowed to play with the other kids in the neighborhood. She wouldn't let me go to their homes, and they weren't allowed to come to my house. If my mother saw some of the kids in our yard, she would chase them away. And that would lead to teasing at school the next day. I was also teased a lot because of my last name. They would yodel at me or ask me if I could yodel. Although it was harmless teasing, it always annoyed me.

Carolyn Odle was an only child, the daughter of strict and conservative parents who reportedly set rigid limits on her social activities. She was born in 1946 and grew up in the postwar era of opportunity, economic expansion, and growing social awareness. The household was dominated by her father, who restricted her social development by placing extreme limitations on her activities and refusing to allow her to participate in school activities outside the classroom or extracurricular activities of any kind. She was rarely allowed to attend social events or visit the homes of her classmates. Conversely, Carolyn's mother was a relatively passive and submissive woman who capitulated to her husband with regard to the household rules and parenting of their daughter. If Carolyn resisted the strict control of her father or violated his oppressive rules, she would be punished.

Years later, Carolyn's best friend, Yvonne Sexton, provided some insight regarding Carolyn's psychological makeup: "Carolyn's father was an alcoholic. She didn't trust people. She was afraid of her dad. I think she was probably abused" (personal communication, September 30, 2006). On one occasion, when Carolyn was a teenager still in high school, a boy walked her home from school and kissed her good-bye while they were standing on her front porch. Her father, who had been watching from inside the house, immediately pulled the boy inside and demanded to know the nature of his relationship with his daughter. Had the physical contact between his daughter and the boy gone beyond kissing? Despite repeated denials from both Carolyn and the boy about any sexual activity and their claims of a completely innocent relationship, her father insisted they get married. Carolyn was made to feel that she had done something horribly wrong by allowing the boy to kiss her and that such behavior was unacceptable, intolerable, and unclean. The two teenagers were married shortly thereafter. The boy was Robert Odle (Y. Sexton, personal communication, September 30, 2006).

Their first child, Thomas V. Odle, was born on December 20, 1966, when Carolyn was twenty. Carolyn adopted the same strict and oppressive parenting style that her parents had used with her. Robert was a shy and quiet man who deferred to his wife with the day-to-day issues and responsibilities of parenting. Like many young mothers, Carolyn struggled with the demands of her new role. She was an emotionally detached woman of rigid character whose knowledge of childcare and parenting was limited to her own restrictive and oppressive upbringing. As a result of the social isolation imposed upon her during childhood, her opportunities to observe different styles of parenting were extremely limited, and her awareness of the dynamics of parent-child relationships was in many ways confined to the dysfunctional relationships within her own family.

With regard to Carolyn's style of parenting, Sexton noted, "I thought it was strange. I often wondered if she was treated the same way she treated her own children; [they were] not allowed to have friends over or go visit other people." She disclosed that on one occasion, she questioned Carolyn as to the reason for her overly protective parenting style: "She said the reason she kept her children home was that they wouldn't get the blame if something happened somewhere. As long as they were home minding their own business, they wouldn't get in any trouble" (personal communication, September 30, 2006).

> I was a good student, and I don't recall getting into any trouble during the younger years, because I was so glad to be out of the house. I don't remember much about my kindergarten year, although like at home, I was by myself a lot. I didn't know any of the kids in my class, since I was not allowed out of my yard and no one was ever allowed in it, either.

I used to hate that so much. The other kids would talk about what they did, like riding minibikes, go-karts, playing sports, or just hanging out. But I was never allowed to do those things, so I was always listening with nothing to say. I wasn't allowed to watch TV back then, either. I was always left out; the last picked.

I started school in 1971, the same year my sister was born. I went to the same school [Horace Mann Elementary] my dad had gone to when he was a boy. I even had the same kindergarten teacher that he had. I was a healthy kid except for a battle with pneumonia that landed me in the hospital for a while. I went to school every day, but I don't remember having any friends in kindergarten.

Former kindergarten classmates of Tom Odle recalled that one morning after he entered the kindergarten classroom, they noticed that the back of his short-sleeved oxford plaid shirt was wet. The classmates brought this to the teacher's attention. She reportedly examined him and lifted the back of his shirt revealing horizontal welts across his back, which was streaked with blood. His shirt was wet with blood that was seeping from the welts, the results of an apparent beating or whipping. The boy reportedly said nothing.

When Tom was five years old, his sister, Robyn, was born.

When my sister was born, I don't think I felt anything for her. We were hardly ever together because I was never allowed out of my room, and she was always in the living room with my mother. And, of course, that was something I did not like. . . . I didn't understand that my sister needed the attention from my mother because she was so young at the time. I just saw her as someone getting to do things I was never allowed to do. Thinking back now, I know I used to think about what my sister was doing and get mad. Then, I'd start playing loudly, and my mom would come in and beat me with a belt or an extension cord, or whatever else was handy. My grandma always told me that when I was little, I wouldn't leave my sister alone. Like, she would be sleeping, and I would wake her up. But I don't remember that; just something I've always been told. I never felt any connection to her or my mother.

Carolyn delivered her second child, Robyn, on September 24, 1971. Carolyn was delighted with Robyn. She now had the daughter she always wanted. Tom, like most boys, was a handful. And, he unfortunately possessed some of Carolyn's personality traits, which resulted in frequent clashes and conflicts between them. Specifically, Tom was strong-willed, obstinate, defiant, and, at times, rebellious. But Tom had started school and was out of her hair much of the time. So she could focus her attention on Robyn and nurture her daughter in a way that was very different and much more fulfilling than her relationship with her son.

However, within four months of Robyn's birth, Carolyn was pregnant, again. She wasn't pleased. Her pregnancy with Robyn was filled with thoughtful anticipation and hopeful expectation. She viewed another pregnancy so soon after Robyn as an unwelcome burden. When she was informed that she would have another son, she was very disappointed. In fact, she was resentful. Tom was difficult. Robyn was a blessing. Now, she was going to have to deal with another Tom.

When Tom was six years old, his brother Sean was born.

> I'll never forget my mother standing in the driveway telling the neighbor that she hated my brother before he was even born. I never knew it until many years later, but at that time she even had me hating him before he was born.

Robert Odle provided little assistance to Carolyn in the day-to-day responsibilities of childrearing. And, for the most part, that was fine with her. Bob was a good man, and she loved him. He worked hard, and he was a solid, reliable provider for the family. But his passive nature and easygoing demeanor frustrated her at times, particularly when it came to the children. Her parents had taught her how to raise children. On one hand, a parent must protect children from the unsavory influences of the world outside the home. On the other hand, children needed discipline. Discipline meant punishment—swift, harsh punishment. That was how children learned right from wrong.

> I only saw my dad on weekends because of his working hours. He worked from four to midnight. So, when I was walking in from school, he was leaving for work. I hated that because I was always left with my mom, playing alone. When my dad was around, he would call me out to the garage, where he would spend his weekends doing odd jobs. And he always

took me everywhere he went. I hated for the weekends to end because I would be left alone, once more, with Her.

There was a mentally challenged girl who lived next door to us. She was about eight or ten years older than me. She was the only one I was allowed to play with. We would play catch, shoot basketball, and play with Matchbox cars. But, if anyone in my class found out, I'd get teased for playing with her.

In addition to the descriptions of sadistic treatment and abusive behavior that were disclosed during the murder trial of Tom Odle, the use of corporal punishment as a standard method of discipline within the Odle household was also revealed by mental-health experts.

I was beaten a lot as a child for playing too loud. By "playing loud," I mean the sound of a toy car rolling across the floor; any sound would, at times, set her off like a firecracker. She would kick and beat me. She would also whip me with belts, extension cords, and Hot Wheels tracks; from my back down to the back of my legs. If I left the yard, I would be beaten right there on the spot. Or, I'd be beaten if I had someone over playing in the yard. I always had marks on my body, but I didn't dare show anybody because it would only make things worse. She would always say, "Whatever happens in the house stays in the house, or else."

Whenever she beat me, she would keep beating me until she got tired, and then she would stop and walk away. So, most of the time all I could do was ball up and try my best to protect myself because it came without warning and would last a while, depending on her stamina at that moment. As I got older, I would take the beatings for my siblings and even got in trouble on purpose just to get beaten because it was a form of attention from my mother. If she wasn't hitting me or yelling at me, she never spoke to me, or I to her.

I was often beaten for lying because I wanted to avoid getting beaten for something I'd done. So, I lied. But I eventually realized that I'd get beaten, regardless. As I got older, the beatings didn't faze me.

Then came the beatings that were combined with her hateful proclamations: "I hope you die; I'm sorry I ever

brought you into this world; I'm sorry to have had a child that
turned out like you." She'd say what a huge disappointment
we all were to her and how she should run off and leave us to
fend for ourselves, and then change her identity. When people
would call the house, my mother would ask why they were
messing with me because I would never amount to anything.

Capital Punishment

As Tom Odle was struggling with his home life, another kind of struggle
was taking place that would dramatically affect his future.

In 1972, when he was still in kindergarten, the U.S. Supreme Court
abolished all state capital-punishment laws. In its review of *Furman v.
Georgia*, 408 U.S. 238 (1972), the Court made this decision based on the
capriciousness and racial discrimination perceived in the case. In 1967,
during his first statement to the police, William Henry Furman said that
he was burgling a house and was surprised by the owner. While trying
to escape, he turned and fired, killing the victim. Furman was a twenty-
six-year-old African American with a sixth-grade education who turned
to petty theft when he couldn't find work. A state-appointed psychiatrist
pronounced him emotionally disturbed and mentally impaired (*Furman
v. Georgia*, 1972).

During his trial in 1968, in an unsworn statement allowed under Georgia's criminal procedure, Furman said that as he fled the scene, he tripped,
and the weapon discharged accidentally, killing the victim. He was tried
for murder and, largely based on his own statements, convicted and sentenced to death (Wikipedia, 2011d).

Regardless of the facts, because the shooting occurred during the commission of a felony, Furman would have been guilty of murder and eligible
for the death penalty under then-extant state law. But when the Supreme
Court reviewed the case, it was determined that the death penalty was the
type of "cruel and unusual punishment" identified by the Eighth Amendment and "incompatible with the evolving standards of decency of contemporary society." Though Furman was armed during the attempted
robbery, the killing more aptly fit the description of manslaughter or in-
voluntary manslaughter. The Court also felt Furman's psychological and
emotional state deserved consideration. Justice Potter Stewart explained
that the Eighth Amendment "cannot tolerate the infliction of a sentence
of death under legal systems that permit this unique penalty to be so
wantonly and so freakishly imposed" (*Furman v. Georgia*, 1972).

After serving sixteen years in prison, Furman was paroled in April 1984.

The Electric Chair

As Tom Odle was growing up, a storm of controversy surrounding the death penalty was already brewing. Up until 1962, the death penalty was carried out by means of electrocution in Illinois. Between 1928 and 1962, ninety-eight executions by electrocution were completed in Illinois ("Electric Chair," 2010). Alfred P. Southwick, a dentist, first developed the idea of execution by electricity after seeing an intoxicated man touch an exposed terminal on a live generator and die instantly. The device became a chair because Southwick was a dentist and was accustomed to working on people in chairs. After a particularly gruesome and bloody hanging was reported, New York State was looking for an alternative to hanging. The first electric chair was manufactured by an employee of Thomas Edison in 1889. The first state-sanctioned electrocution took place in 1890. It took eight minutes (Wikipedia, 2011b).

Although electric chairs varied in size and style, the process for execution was the same. The condemned person's head and legs were shaved, and then he or she was strapped to the chair. A moist sponge was placed on the head to help ensure conductivity. To create a closed circuit, one electrode was attached to the head and the other to the shaved area on the leg. The prisoner received at least two jolts of electric current. The length of time and level of current depended on the prisoner's size, but the typical first jolt was 2,000 volts for fifteen seconds. That was usually enough time and enough power to render the person unconscious. Then the voltage was lowered, and current flow was reduced to finish the job. The condemned's body heat rose to around 138 degrees, and the electric current damaged the internal organs (Wikipedia, 2011b).

Cleanup was unpleasant. Burnt skin had to be removed from the electrodes. The condemned usually lost control of all natural body functions. Loss of consciousness usually occurred in a fraction of a second. But in multiple cases, that did not happen, and there were well-documented reports of screaming and hair and clothing burning. Ultimately, these reports and their subsequent legal actions led to the wide-scale demise of the electric chair for capital punishment.

On August 24, 1962, in the basement of the Cook County Jail in Chicago, James Dukes became the last prisoner to be electrocuted by the State of Illinois. Dukes, an African American, was convicted of killing a police detective. The detective was killed trying to arrest Dukes for shooting two men who were trying to stop him from beating a woman (U.S. Court of Appeals Seventh Circuit, 1962). After the execution of James Dukes in 1962, there were no executions in Illinois for twenty-eight years.

In fact, by the time Dukes was strapped in the electric chair, public sentiment had begun to shift away from the death penalty. In 1966, support for capital punishment in the United States reached an all-time low, with only 42 percent in favor, according to a Gallup poll (Bohm, 1999). Capital punishment was suspended in 1967 to allow the appeals courts to decide whether the death penalty was unconstitutional. This ultimately led to the *Furman v. Georgia* decision in 1972. As a result of the Furman decision, combined with the long and arduous appeals process in most capital cases, the State of Illinois would not resume executions until September 12, 1990, with the execution of Charles Walker, five years after the Odle family murders. He had been convicted of the double murder of a couple in East Saint Louis in 1983 and sentenced to death. Walker's was the first execution in Illinois in nearly three decades (Center on Wrongful Convictions, 2011).

2

Discipline, Deprivation, and Resentment

The house I grew up in was built sometime in the 40s, maybe earlier. That's when that part of town was built. It was a basic box-style house. During the 70s, rooms were added on to try to keep up with the growing family.

The basic décor was that of the 70s: multi-colored carpeting and furniture. That is when everything was purchased except for the living room audio-visual stuff, which was purchased in the early 80s. So, the furniture was outdated, but the stereo equipment was new.

The house was small for 6 people. It was crammed full of furniture. The living room was small but had a couch, two recliners, a TV, and stereo. That left room for little else. The master bedroom had a queen-sized bed, a chest of drawers, and a dresser with a mirror. There was very little room to walk around. The kitchen was over-crowded with a table that seated 6 people but was made for 4 on a good day. The table stretched from the dining room to the kitchen and there was barely enough room to get through the back door. The den was filled with a loveseat, a huge desk, a sewing machine, an enormous bookcase stuffed with books, old tube-styled radios, and knick-knacks. I shared a bedroom with my two brothers. The room was stuffed with three twin beds, a dresser, and an entertainment center. My sister's bedroom had barely anything in it: a full-sized bed, a TV, a chest of drawers, and that was it. That's where my siblings hung out because of the space.

We tried to move several times, but the house wouldn't sell. It was located in an elderly neighborhood where young people didn't [stay] for very long. Our neighborhood had lots of sort-of-like starter homes for newly married people until they got on their feet, solidly. But my parents bought the house because it was close to my paternal grandparents, an uncle, and a cousin. They all lived a block or two from one another.

I started getting into trouble a little bit during my first-grade year. I was the kid who, if dared to do something, would do it regardless of the outcome. I just wanted to be liked and accepted by the kids in my school.

My brother Sean was born that year. So then, it was me, my sister, Robyn, and my brother Sean. I was put in charge of taking care of him for the most part. When I came home from school, it became my job to feed him, change his diapers, and everything else he needed, because she hated him so much. I used to hate it, and I'd always wonder why she wouldn't do it, as it was her baby and her job, not mine. She took care of my sister, so why not Sean, also?

I never spoke up to my mom when I was little because I was always scared of her. If Sean cried for any reason, I'd get whipped because I was not to let him bother her. Nor was I to bother her. I bathed Sean. I did everything a parent is supposed to do. And I did it when I was six years old. I know it wasn't his fault that he was born, but at that time, I blamed Sean for that. And I hated him just like my mother did.

Family Dynamics and Parenting Techniques

Sean Odle was born on October 7, 1972. Fourteen years later, during the sentencing phase of Tom's murder trial, the Odles' next-door neighbor Maurice Yeargin testified that Carolyn Odle told his wife "when she was carrying Sean, she hated him and she hated him from then on. After he was born, she hated him. She encouraged all the kids to hate him. None of the kids liked him." He also told the court that Tom was commonly left in charge of the other children and that Carolyn told him that "her doctor told her she had nerves. She should go out every night and [it would] be good for her. She should leave Tommy to babysit with the kids. It would be good for him." He also stated that Tom was particularly rough with Sean, and he was often mean to him. However, he added that all members of the family were mean to Sean (*People of the State of Illinois vs. Thomas Odle*, 1986).

When her children were younger, Carolyn was content to stay at home. Robyn, in Carolyn's view, was a good girl, and Carolyn loved spending time with her daughter. Tom, on the other hand, was too smart for his own good and just as stubborn and strong willed as Carolyn. Tom knew how to push her buttons, and she resented him for it. She had punished him many times, and yet, he continued to misbehave, talk back, and violate the rules of the house. Then Sean came along. She viewed him as little more than a nuisance and did not want to be bothered with his needs. Tom was available to take care of Sean and would see to Sean's needs whether Tom liked it or not. Why shouldn't a mother expect her oldest child to assist her in caring for the younger children? So, as Tom grew older, Carolyn assigned him increasing responsibilities with regard to the other children. After all, by the time he was nine or ten, she felt he was capable of babysitting the younger kids.

Family dynamics are crucial to understanding the motives behind acts of familicide. After the birth of his sister, Tom's relationship with his mother changed significantly. Robyn's need for maternal care and Carolyn's desire to nurture her daughter, while providing less attention to Tom, fostered a growing sense of rejection and isolation in the boy. As he grew older, his conflicted relationship with his mother worsened. He sought attention by rebellious acts of defiance and aggression. He was frequently in fights with other boys at school. As a result, teachers often called Carolyn to inform her of the fights and elicit her assistance in managing Tom's behavior. Margie Long and Sid Milliner, teachers at Horace Mann Elementary School in Mt. Vernon, recalled that Carolyn would adamantly defend Tom and insist that he should not be held responsible for such behavior because he was merely protecting himself and simply reacting to the frequent bullying by the other boys (M. Long, personal communication, June 16, 2006; S. Milliner, personal communication, June 16, 2006).

Elementary School and Social Isolation

I was still making the average grades; nothing outstanding. The teachers would tell my parents that I needed to apply myself. I studied very little and easily made a C average. I couldn't please my parents when it came to my grades. My dad didn't say very much, just that he knew I could do better.

But my mother would say I was stupid if I got a B. If I made straight A's, then she would say that I should be getting A's all the time. So, I would get whipped for making less than straight A's, and I'd get whipped for making straight A's. It didn't matter what grades I made because I was going to get whipped either way. I hated report card day. I also started hating school, but I was too scared not to go.

I was allowed to start walking home from school at about that time because we only lived about five blocks from the school. If I was a minute late, I'd get the third degree about where I had been and what took me so long to get home. I was not allowed to participate in any activities after school, so I was still isolated from my classmates. I wanted to fit in, but I never did. You know, in school when everybody gets their picture taken and then they exchange pictures. I was never asked to exchange pictures with anybody. When my mom would give me pictures to take to school, I ended up throwing them away because nobody asked me and I was too ashamed to tell anyone.

My summers were always the same; playing by myself and being told to stay out of the house and leave her alone. Sometimes she would lock me out of the house. But when Sean would cry, she would let me in to take care of him. Otherwise, I would be kicked back outside to play alone each and every day of the summer. Sometimes, I'd play with the girl next door, but not too often. My dad didn't really approve. But sometimes my mom would come out and tell her degrading things about me, right in front of me; call me names and say how stupid I was. What could I say? I was nothing to her.

Every time I did something wrong I was told how much she hated ever having me and that she wished she had never had me. She would say that she wished I would die and be gone from her, because I wasn't wanted. All my life I heard that from her, ever since I can remember. According to her, I was a failure as a son; I was stupid. She would say, "Why don't you die. Please run away so I won't have to deal with you." I heard these things from the time I was in grade school until I was a teenager. I never felt love from that woman, at all.

We were at a church Christmas party, and I had to get up with the choir and sing carols. When it was over, I got whipped because she said I looked stupid up there and wasn't singing right. She always embarrassed me by whipping me in front of everybody. My dad would never stop her or tell her to wait, or nothing. He said nothing at all. I always used to look for my dad to say something to her about it, but he never did.

Second grade was much the same as first grade. I always liked gym because it was forced team participation and I couldn't be ignored. Otherwise, I always felt ignored by everyone. My sister continued to get all of the attention from my mother. We had added a new addition to the house, so Sean and I had to share a room, while my sister got her own room. The only thing I ever had for enjoyment was jigsaw puzzles, books, and I used to draw a lot. When I'd no longer cry when I was whipped, I would not only get whipped, but I would lose something that meant something to me. I would lose my jigsaw puzzle or my drawing stuff, or my books.

During the second grade, I had my first girlfriend. And, I had my first kiss then. But when she gave me a ring, my mom told me I had to give it back and that I couldn't be her boyfriend. So, I gave it back to her. Then, later on that day, this other guy had it on his finger, and he shoved it in my face to show me that he was now her "boyfriend." Maybe she was right to make me give it back, but what harm could it have caused; a ring from a girl in the second grade?

When I was about to go into the third grade, my mom started taking me to this new church by our house. It was a Baptist church, and I really liked it there. I had never really been to church, before. I was baptized then, and I started reading the Bible. I was also involved in a youth group. I was having a good time. It was something new and a place where everyone accepted everyone else. There was niceness and I guess what one would call love there at that church. Plus, the pastor lived up the street from us at that time. I was still taking care of my brother Sean, which had become second nature to me by then. Also, my sister started hanging around me more at that time, and my mom would actually tell my sister not to hang around me because I was a bad influence.

In the third grade I remember my teacher because I used to think she was the prettiest teacher ever; brunette hair, green eyes. I used to love to go to school then. My mom knew her dad because he was a doctor where my mom went for her prenatal care. I remember school being fun, then. And things seemed better at home, too. I wonder if it had to do with church. Or was it because I was growing up? My sister was growing up, and we were hanging out more, so I wasn't alone anymore.

I even had a friend in school that year by the name of Stan. He was my first real friend. We would go to each other's home, and I finally felt the grip lessening from my mom, because I had a friend who would come over and I would go over there. I had even joined a Cub Scout Unit through the church and was a part of that. I worked hard and earned a lot of the Cub Scout awards. Stan was also a part of the Cub Scout Unit. We remained friends most of the year, but it ended when we got into a fistfight at school over something. I can't even recall what it was about. But I know I got in trouble at home because his parents called my parents and made my mom cry. So, of course, I got whipped for that. And afterwards, my mom went back to not letting anyone come over to the house, and once again, I couldn't go to anyone's house, either. Every time I asked to go anywhere or have someone come over, the answer would be "no." So, after a while, I just stopped asking.

Effects of Verbal Abuse

During this stage of Tom's life, the abuse by his mother became more complex and damaging psychologically. Previously, her abusive acts primarily involved beatings, whippings, isolation, and exclusion from the home. During his preadolescent years, the physical abuse was accompanied and sometimes replaced by verbal abuse. In some ways, recurrent hateful verbal abuse of a child by a parent is more emotionally disturbing and psychologically damaging than physical abuse. Physical abuse tends to instill a sense of fear and insecurity. Verbal abuse, on the other hand, is a direct attack on the child's self-concept, and recurrent hostile verbal abuse by a parent, involving insulting and degrading statements to a young child, may be expected to have a disruptive and destructive impact on emotional development and personality formation. An early manifestation of this type of destructive impact involves aggressive acting-out behaviors with other children at school.

The aggressive tendencies that Tom began manifesting during his early elementary-school years were likely the result of several factors, including the following: venting frustration and anger he felt toward his mother, seeking attention from his peers and teachers, and copying the behavior of his primary role model, his mother. Like most elementary-school children, Tom had teachers whom he liked and those he did not particularly like. He developed a crush on his third-grade teacher because he thought she was pretty, but he also admittedly disliked other teachers because they insisted that he behave himself or because they demanded that he try harder, with respect to his schoolwork.

Unfortunately, due to his mother's parenting style, he apparently had limited opportunities for social and interpersonal experiences outside of the home or school. With few exceptions, he was generally not allowed to visit the homes of children from school, and he wasn't allowed to play with other children in his neighborhood. And, his classmates were generally not allowed to visit the Odle home. Additionally, he was not allowed to spend the night at a classmate's house, and other children were not allowed to spend the night at the Odle house.

In part, as a result of the forced social isolation and psychological abuse by his mother at home, Tom's behavioral problems escalated at school.

> I think it was about that time I started getting into a lot of fights at school because I was tired of being picked on. So, instead of debating back and forth, I just fought back with my fists, like I had been doing all my life, or so it seemed. And of course, I would get in trouble at school for fighting. Back in those days, they would give you swats with a board for misbehaving, and then I would get it at home, also.
>
> My parents would always ask me why I was fighting. I would tell them that "they called me names" or "they were talking about my mom or dad." My parents would tell me to "let it go in one ear and out the other." But when you're little and tired of being picked on all the time, fighting just seems like the next step. I got suspended a few times for fighting. And if I got into a fight, I better have won, because if I hadn't, I would get whipped worse at home for losing. I didn't win them all, but I didn't lose very many. I wonder why I can't remember anything good about those times, because I know

there had to be some. It couldn't have all been bad, but I can't remember anything good.

Years later, Milliner shared his perception regarding Tom's aggressive tendencies and deceptiveness: "Tommy was always argumentative. He always thought he was right in whatever he was doing. Whenever he got in trouble, Mommy was the first one there to defend him, and it seemed like she was always taking his side. He'd pick a fight with one of the kids on the playground; the other kid wouldn't start the fight. But by the time Mommy got there, he'd say the other kid was picking on him. And it would be that way every time" (personal communication, June 16, 2006).

Jerry Clemens, the principal of Horace Mann Elementary School, also frequently dealt with Carolyn, as a result of Tom's disruptive behavior at school: "It always seemed to me that she was defending Tommy to save her own face. It was well practiced on her part. I don't remember Tommy from the younger ages, but I remember his ability to look you in the eye and tell you something he knew you knew wasn't fact. Carolyn herself was about the most severe case of denial that you could possibly imagine. She put forward quite a little persona of being interested in the kids, but she was pretty manipulative herself. I really think she had Robert wrapped around her finger, and he really didn't see it. Never saw it coming. I think she definitely wore the pants in the family. He didn't have the slightest inkling. Couldn't fathom it, maybe. He was a hard-working, decent guy and probably well liked on his job. I can't say that about Carolyn. I think she had one friend" (personal communication, June 16, 2006).

> When I started the fourth grade, I never got along with the teacher, because I always thought she was after me. Later on I found out that she was just after me to do better because she knew I could do it. I learned everything fast, without any problem.
>
> The only time I was really happy was when I was in church with my dad or my grandparents. I'm sure my mom would do nice things for me or with me, but I can't remember them. I remember going fishing with my parents, sometimes, and that was good. I also recall us having picnics, but for the most part, we never did much as a family. My parents went on vacations by themselves and left us with our grandparents.
>
> Even when we ate dinner on Sundays, we would eat after my parents had eaten. My mom would cook a huge

> dinner, and my parents would eat while the food was hot. But
> we [the children] always ate the food, cold. And, of course, I
> was always the kitchen help: keeping the kitchen clean, doing
> dishes, the floor, and table. I would get so pissed off because I
> felt like I was her slave, or something. And, I wouldn't receive
> any allowance, like everyone else my age seemed to be get-
> ting. I also had to take out the garbage and mow the yard. I
> know that kids have chores to do and that is part of growing
> up, but in my mind, I always thought I was doing too much
> and that I was some sort of slave around the house.

Twenty years after the murder of his family, Tom Odle's recollection of his life from age six to about ten reveals a dynamic within the Odle household that is typical of dysfunctional families with an abusive element. At a very young age, Tom's brother Sean became the family scapegoat. As such, he was the target of unwarranted blame and ongoing physical and mental abuse throughout his short life. The disdain that Carolyn felt toward Sean was projected to Tom, and he admittedly came to hate Sean, much like his mother did.

When Tom was nine years old, his second brother, Scott, was born.

> My brother Scott was born in 1975 right after I started the
> fourth grade. I really didn't have any connection with Robyn
> or Sean because they were so much younger than me. They
> started hanging around each other a lot, and as Sean got
> older, he started taking care of himself. Then Scott came
> along. I really thought nothing of it, but after some time
> passed I realized there was something different about him.
> It's difficult to describe, but we were cool from the start.
> About the same time though, my brother Sean started doing
> stuff around the house that my mom would call "stealing
> food." It was weird. He would get up in the middle of the
> night to get a snack. And my mom would get bent out of
> shape about it, as if someone had stolen all of her money.

The U.S. Constitution and the Illinois Death Penalty

In 1973, while Tom Odle was in the first grade, a crime was committed in Georgia that would ultimately impact his life. On November 21, 1973, Troy Gregg and Floyd Allen were hitchhiking through northern Florida. They were picked up by Fred Simmons and Bob Moore, who were driving north to Georgia. Later that night, near Atlanta, Gregg robbed and killed both Simmons and Moore in an execution-style, double murder. Gregg was convicted of murder and sentenced to death, based on Georgia's new statutory scheme. That scheme was developed following the *Furman v. Georgia* decision, which found the former death-penalty statute unconstitutional, resulting in a de facto moratorium on executions in the United States (*Gregg v. Georgia*, 1976; Wikipedia, 2011f).

At about the same time, as a result of the Furman ruling, Illinois legislators were forced to reformulate the state's death-penalty statute. By November 1973, then-governor Dan Walker signed a new Illinois death penalty into law only to see it voided by the Illinois Supreme Court in 1975 because it was considered unconstitutional (Center for Wrongful Convictions, 2011).

In 1976, when ten-year-old Tom Odle was in the fourth grade, the U.S. Supreme Court approved Georgia's rewritten death-penalty statute under which Gregg was sentenced to death. The Court's finding that the death sentence delivered in *Gregg v. Georgia*, along with two other death-penalty cases (*Jurek v. Texas* and *Proffit v. Florida*), was constitutional served to reinstate the death penalty in the United States (*Gregg v. Georgia*, 1976; Wikipedia, 2011f).

In June 1977, a revised death-penalty statute was initiated by Illinois legislators and upheld by the Illinois Supreme Court in 1979. Despite the fact that a minority of dissenters held that the new statute was unconstitutional, due to its lack of guidelines to prevent the arbitrary exercise of discretion by prosecutors, the State of Illinois now had a death-penalty law on the books (Center for Wrongful Convictions, 2011). Tom Odle was thirteen years old.

Shortly after the implementation of the revised Illinois death-penalty statute, another case was tried that would have a dramatic impact on Tom Odle's future. Darby Tillis and Perry Cobb were convicted of the double murder of the owner and an employee of a hotdog stand in Chicago and sentenced to death. However, in January 1987, one year after the Odle family murders, they were acquitted based on the testimony of an assistant state's attorney who was aware that the two had been convicted based on the false testimony of the girlfriend of the actual killer. Tillis and Cobb would be the first two in a long line of men wrongfully convicted of murder in Illinois who would ultimately be exonerated after many years on death row (Center on Wrongful Convictions, 2011).

3

Beatings, Chains, and Fifth Grade

All four of the Odle children attended Horace Mann Elementary School. The building was typical for its era: a brown-and-beige-brick structure with a strip of windows in every classroom, tile floors, and hallways lined by lockers, and all activity underscored by the steady hum of fluorescent lighting.

Squeals, shoe squeaks, and the thundering bounces of balls filled the halls when the gym doors opened. Ladies wearing hairnets served lunch from steam tables. The classrooms smelled like chalk dust, pencil shavings, and the ink in ballpoint pens. The classrooms themselves were drab affairs. Teachers were encouraged to fill them with color: posters, photos, mobiles, and sculpture, anything that might stimulate the increasingly shorter adolescent attention span.

It was a time when America was, in part, defined by *All in the Family*, *MASH*, *Happy Days*, longer hair on men, pet rocks and mood rings, platform shoes and leisure suits, disco and *Star Wars.* America was embracing these gaudy images that were reflective of its cultural values. And, as it is with all fads and trends, those who did not embrace that mainstream norm were considered to be outsiders.

Socially, Tom continually felt like an outsider throughout his childhood.

> When I was ten, I used to dance in the morning before
> school with these two girls, Tanya, who had been my friend
> for many years, and another girl, Toni. I really don't know
> why I remember Toni now, after all these years. I guess I

remember her because she accepted me for who I was. I always thought that the other kids had a better understanding of what was going on during childhood, because I never got to do very much with other kids my age. I always felt isolated and stupid when I made mistakes, as far as etiquette, when I was around other kids my own age.

I was in a fight with one of the cool kids, and I beat him up pretty bad. After that, he wasn't so cool anymore, and a lot more kids talked to me and included me in activities at school, such as softball, dodgeball, and basketball. I even got invited to several birthday parties. But I never went to any of them because my mother wouldn't allow me to go. So again, I was slowly faded out, and eventually the other kids no longer asked me to do anything because they knew I wouldn't be allowed to go. That really hurt me.

My mother always talked about how she had been excluded from most things when she was young because her parents were so strict. But, instead of letting me socialize with my peers, I was made to suffer the same fate as my mother. She also seemed to need to deprive me of most things. Once, my father built a minibike for me, with an old lawnmower engine. When my mother found out about it, she sold the minibike. That caused a huge rift between my mother and father. I guess I never really forgave her for a lot of the things she made me endure when I was a child.

There was a time in the fourth grade when I had to write a paper. I wrote about how much I wasn't wanted at home and how out of place I felt. I ended up getting some swats at school because they thought I was lying and playing games with them. Then, of course, they told my mom who beat me for writing something like that. She told me, "Whatever goes on in this house, stays in this house." I sometimes wonder if that paper had been taken seriously at school, would something have been done to help out my family. Why was it looked upon as a joke? Why did I need to be punished for it? But that was the 70s instead of now, when things like that are taken more seriously.

I was beginning to be the class clown about that time, also. I found that I could make people laugh, and if I did stuff to make them laugh, they would like me. So, I got into some trouble here and there by messing up the classroom or making funny noises, drawing funny pictures; anything for a laugh and recognition from my peers.

I was never the best student, but I could have been if I had applied myself. Even Tanya, my *dancing partner,* used to get mad at me because I didn't apply myself. I would help her with her homework and not even do my own homework, because I just didn't want to. Half the time I didn't do any homework just because I didn't care. I knew that whether I did it or not, I was going to get ridiculed or whipped for it.

So, I would get in trouble when the baby wouldn't stop crying because I couldn't keep him quiet. Then, I would get in trouble when the report cards came out. And I'd get in trouble for being the class clown. During that time I was getting whipped a lot, and a lot of things were being taken away from me. At one point, I didn't get any Christmas presents because I was so bad, and I had to watch everyone else open presents. I wasn't going to church any longer either because I had that taken away from me for the writing incident at school.

While I was in the fourth grade, my paternal grandpa died. I really loved my grandpa. It was the first time I ever went to a funeral or a wake. And, it was the only time I ever saw my dad cry. I remember when it happened because everybody went over to my grandma's house, and I found out a lot of things that day. I found out that nobody on my father's side of the family liked my mom. That was why they never came over to our house anymore. It was because of the way she had been treating me and Sean, and they were mad at my dad for not taking a stronger stand against her.

I remember my cousin used to come over and play with me when I was little. She was about five or six years younger than my parents. One time, she saw my mom start smacking me for no particular reason, and she had to stop her. Then, my mom got mad at her for interfering, and she never came around again. Of course the gossip spread about what she had seen, and it caused a huge break in my dad's side of the family. Anyway, my mom took us over to my grandma's house, but nobody would talk to her. They just waited for my dad to come over. I look back now and wonder why they feel the way they do about me, since they did nothing to stop it.

At about that time, I saw the light in my grandma's eyes go out. The sparkle she had in her eyes was gone when my grandpa died. She was never the same. It wasn't until I got older that I began to realize what happened in '76 that caused her eyes to die. I don't know if I ever want to feel that pain that she had to endure when my grandpa died. I always felt lost after my grandpa died and my grandma changed because they were the people with whom I felt wanted and needed, unlike at home.

I remember my grandpa telling me about death and heaven, and stuff like that. I knew about it, but I had never experienced it, and to this day, I wonder if he can see me and what he must think of me. I wonder if he would understand, or if he would turn his back on me like the rest of the family. My dad was never the same after his father died. He was more subdued, and just like my grandma, seemingly dead inside.

At the age of forty, Tom Odle reflected on his experiences and relationships from age ten to fourteen. Peer acceptance is common to the developmental stage of early adolescence. But in Tom's case, the normal concerns and insecurities of early adolescence seem to have been aggravated by the social restrictions and isolation that his mother imposed on him. As a result of the physical and emotional abuse at home, at least in part, his aggressive acting-out behaviors outside the home increased significantly during this period. At the same time, he was beginning to realize that the abuse to which he had become accustomed was considered inappropriate and unacceptable by other people.

When I was in the fifth grade, I had a teacher whom I remember very fondly because I had a crush on her. She was beautiful; long red hair and green eyes. I was also a bit more accepted by my class in the fifth grade because of the goofing off. But I also had to contend with this hair thing. Most people in my class had long hair, as it was the '70s. But I always had to wear a crew cut that my dad gave me. I would get laughed at whenever I got a haircut. I hated haircuts, which is one of the reasons I wear my hair so long most of the time now. I just wanted to blend in with everyone else. It seemed that I fit in better when my hair was growing out and not so short. But once it got cut, the ridicule started again. And when it got bad, the fights would start.

I started playing baseball in an organized league about that time. I think they called it little minor league baseball. I really had a blast. I always liked playing catcher and third base because they seemed to be the hot spots. I collected baseball cards for years and would listen to the ball games with my grandpa out in the yard, before he died. I was a huge Cardinal fan, and I wanted to grow up and play baseball for the Cardinals. The one time my father came to one of my games, I hit a home run over the fence. It was the only time either of them ever saw me play ball. My mom would take me, drop me off, and then leave. But I really didn't care because I was playing baseball. Baseball made everything all right. That was a good year for me. I had a cute teacher who I thought I was going to grow up and marry. And, I was playing baseball.

During that time my brother was still "stealing food" at night for which he got all the whippings. And, my mom would deny him food, also. That was another one of her punishments; being sent to bed without any dinner after having to sit there and watch everyone else eat. I tried to take the heat off him by taking some of the blame in order to save him from being whipped and made to go hungry. I hated him in one sense because I had to take care of him. But on the other hand, I couldn't stand by and let my mom beat him like she did, and not do something about it. So, I would take the blame when I could. But eventually, it got to the point where she would just punish both of us when something came up missing. My sister was never into anything because she was always hanging around my mom or playing with my brothers. I don't think I ever saw her get whipped or anything, except for a couple of times when we all had to be punished because my mom couldn't decide which one of us should be punished for something.

I think it was about that time that I started shoplifting at the local mom and pop grocery store. I would steal little things like candy bars, sodas, gum, and kid stuff because the other kids always had that stuff, but I was never allowed to

have it. So, I would take it from the store. I would also steal
things that my mom told me to buy for her and keep the
money she had given to me because I wasn't given an allow-
ance and never had any money of my own. I got caught a few
times, but since it was the neighborhood grocery store, they
would always turn me loose. They would tell me not to do it
again, give it back, and get out of there.

Chained to a Bed

Shoplifting adolescents are hardly an anomaly. It is a relatively normal
part of childhood to test the boundaries of the adult world, to discover
what the real rules are, where the firm limitations lie, and determine
what we can get away with: smoking cigarettes, experimenting with drugs
and alcohol, exploring pornography, or shoplifting. We are tempted by
the forbidden fruits of adulthood, and we pursue that temptation. But
there was a strong undercurrent at work in Tom Odle's life: a series of
events and circumstances that were part of being born into his family
that were propelling him along further than the realm of typical adolescent misbehavior. Under the best of circumstances, Tom would have
probably stepped outside the boundaries of normal, acceptable behavior.
That was part of his character, to explore the boundaries and push the
envelope when it came to rules and behavior. But no one could have seen
the eventual outcome of his early attempts to discover his true self and
cope with the perils of his home life.

Six months after the murders, Tom underwent a comprehensive psychological evaluation by Michael Althoff, PhD, at the request of the public
defenders that represented him during his trial. The results of Dr. Althoff's
informed and insightful examination of Tom were used to educate the jury
and the court. He noted, "It appears that there is a long-standing history
of physical and emotional abuse to Tom by his mother. There appears to
have been excessive corporal punishment in addition to unusually cruel
consequences, such as chaining him to the bed. His mother reportedly
also engaged in a number of behaviors that were emotionally cruel and
were geared to inflicting guilt and control through condescension and
criticism. . . . Also, of significant importance is the fact that Tom's perception of his mother was of someone who behaved in inconsistent ways.
This suggests that he viewed his mother as unpredictable and that there
was no stable or constant way in which she related to him" (*People of the
State of Illinois vs. Thomas Odle*, 1986).

As I got older, the beatings stopped [and] were replaced with other forms of abuse, such as chaining me to a bed with a dog chain and padlocks. These new forms of punishment were combined with hateful statements by my mother. She would say that she wished I had never been born. And, she would constantly say what a huge disappointment I was to her as a child. Why was I still alive? Why didn't I run away? She was constantly droning on and on with these mean and hateful words. These were things I always heard almost daily from the woman who gave me life. Sometimes, I wish she had never given me life.

My father had heard her say these things to me many times. And, he even knew that she was chaining me to the bed. But he never stood up for me. And, he never stopped her from beating me, slapping me, or degrading me. He let it all take place. He was always working during the time I wasn't in school, from 4:00 P.M. to 12:00 A.M., so I always had to deal with my mother.

As I got older, I could never understand why he allowed her to do those things. I don't think I could ever sit back and let someone treat my son or daughter in such as manner as that. You don't tell a child that you're sorry you tried so hard to have them and what a disappointment they have turned out to be. I started hearing this when I was about ten or so, along with chaining me to the bed.

Being chained to the bed was something else. At first, she used plastic wire wraps, like the plastic handcuffs they use now. She used them instead of a babysitter so she could go out and do whatever. Before she started with the chaining, she would go out in the evening while my dad was working. After she left, I'd leave, but I always tried to beat her home. When she found out about my activities, she started chaining me to the bed. Then, I started breaking the plastic wire wraps, so she switched to a dog chain.

Unaware of the abuse that went on behind the doors of the Odle home, her friend, Yvonne Sexton, saw another side of Carolyn's complex personality: "I looked up to her. I liked her a lot. I was impressed by her. She was seven years older than me. I met her at the school. She was the PTO president, and I went to all of the PTO meetings, and I played the piano for all of the children's things, and we just got to know each other. I was elected an officer, and we got to be better friends. And also we bowled together later on. We went out bowling once or twice a week. We also went shopping together." But aside from their social activities and the camaraderie that Yvonne shared with her friend, she was perplexed by the manner in which Carolyn would discipline her children in response to minor infractions of the household rules: "She would hit their palms with a paddle. If they would not admit it, all of them would be punished" (personal communication, September 30, 2006).

> The chain went from my bed to the bathroom. It was wrapped around the bed frame with a padlock and the other end was wrapped around my ankle and secured with a padlock. I never asked about her reasoning or where she came up with such an idea. My father knew and he wouldn't stop her or intervene. I was chained 2–4 times per week for a few hours, usually from 6–9 p.m., or so. The chaining began when I was about 9 and ended when I was about 12. It ended because I began using pliers to break the chain and refused to be chained any longer. I also showed my brother how to undo the chain. I guess when you're submitted to that kind of abuse when you're a kid, you don't necessarily think it's bizarre, until you're out of the situation.
>
> My brother Sean . . . would get up at night and eat snacks. My mother called it "stealing food." He would get up at night and eat a sandwich or a cupcake. But we weren't allowed to snack between meals. If we did, my mother would accuse us of stealing food, and we would be forced to skip the next meal. I don't know where the idea came from, but that was why my brother Sean would be chained up all night. She used the same type of dog chain that she used on me. However, Sean was more courageous than me because he eventually told someone at school who believed him.

Child Abuse in the United States

In 1986, when Tom Odle was tried for the murder of his family, the relationship between child abuse and subsequent criminal acts by abused children was not well understood. At that time, two million children were reported as abused with a prevalence rate of 33 per 1,000 children in the U.S. population (American Association for Protecting Children, 1988).

Three years later in 1989, Dr. Cathy Widom, renowned criminologist and expert on the psychological and behavioral effects of child abuse, particularly the relationship between child abuse and criminal behavior later in life, published a seminal article in the prestigious journal *Science* on the long-term effects of child abuse, "The Cycle of Violence" (1989).

Dr. Widom's influential study, involving over nine hundred cases of abuse, reveals that abused and neglected children have more arrests as juveniles, more arrests as adults, and more arrests for violent offenses than their peers who did not suffer abuse. She concludes, "Early childhood victimization has demonstrable long-term consequences for delinquency, adult criminality, and violent criminal behavior." With respect to the hypothesis that violence breeds violence, she found that "physical abuse as a child led significantly to later violent criminal behavior, when other relevant demographic variables such as age, sex, and race were held constant," indicating that abused children have a significantly greater risk of becoming violent criminals. Overall, suffering childhood abuse and neglect increases the odds of future delinquency and adult criminality by 29 percent (1989).

In a follow-up, longitudinal study, Widom and Michael Maxfield (2001) found that being abused or neglected during childhood increases the likelihood of arrest as a juvenile by 59 percent, as an adult by 28 percent, and for a violent crime by 30 percent. Related research by Widom and her colleagues regarding the relationship between child abuse and violent criminal behavior reveals that abuse during childhood significantly increases the likelihood of developing antisocial personality traits and antisocial personality disorder (Perez & Widom, 1994; Widom, 1998).

During the decade from 1986 to 1996, the rate of reported child abuse in the United States increased from 33 to 43.5 per 1000 children in the population, with 22.7 percent suffering physical abuse and 6 percent suffering emotional abuse (U.S. Department of Health and Human Services, 2000). However, many experts believe that the actual rate of child abuse did not increase during that period but rather the rate of reported child abuse increased in response to the implementation of child-abuse-reporting laws. As a result of increased public awareness stemming from the work of social-science researchers like Widom and the implementation of legislation and policies that mandate reporting of suspected abuse to child-protective-service agencies, the rates of reported child abuse subsequently declined.

In striking contrast to his mother's abusive tendencies, Tom's father rarely resorted to physical punishment with his children.

My father wasn't violent or really into punishment of any
kind. He would generally talk to me about what I had done
wrong. No matter how serious the wrong, he was willing to
talk, unless my mother urged him to physically punish one of
us. I only recall two incidents when my father put his hands
on any of us, and it was at the urging of my mother. One
time, my brother had taken some money from my grandmother (my mother's mom), and my father was just talking
to him. My mother started yelling and calling my father soft
and weak. She kept yelling and degrading my father until my
father finally grabbed my brother Sean and started spanking
him really hard with his hand. He kept spanking him for a
long time. I was shocked. When he finally stopped, it seemed
like she was high. She got high by watching him punish my
brother. She seemed thrilled by it. He asked her if that was
"soft and weak."

In 2006, according to the U.S. Department of Health and Human Services
(2011), the rate of child abuse and neglect was 12.1 per 1,000 children in
the population with a total of 905,000 cases of child abuse and neglect in
the United States. Of these children, 16 percent suffered physical abuse,
and 6.6 percent experienced emotional abuse. With regard to the sex of
the victims, 48.2 percent of abused children were boys, and 51.5 percent
were girls. Younger children were more likely to be abused. From birth
to age one, 24.4 per 1,000 children were abused. The rate for ages one
to three was 14.2 per 1,000 children, and from age four to seven, 13.5
per 1,000 children were abused. For victims in the age range of four to
seven, 15.3 percent were physically abused. For victims in the age range
of twelve to fifteen years, 20.1 percent were physically abused. With regard to the relationship between the child and the abuser, 82.4 percent
of children were abused by a parent acting alone or with another person.
A remarkable 40 percent of abused children were abused by their mothers acting alone, whereas only 17.6 percent were abused by their fathers
acting alone.

The only other time my father got physical was when I got
busted for some residential burglaries, and my mother
urged him on, again. He beat me with closed fists. And, he
beat my ass pretty good. We didn't talk for a few weeks until
one day my father apologized. But now, I know that the only

reason he beat me was because my mother urged him on. And by the time I was 14 or so, she had stopped hitting me, herself, because I threw her up against the wall and told her "No More."

Richard Speck and Gary Gilmore

As a result of the U.S. Supreme Court's decision in *Gregg v. Georgia* in 1976, the national moratorium on death sentences ended. The 1972 *Furman v. Georgia* decision kept convicted Chicago-area murderer Richard Speck out of the electric chair. Speck was convicted of the brutal murders of eight student nurses in Chicago in 1966. A ninth student nurse, who stayed hidden during Speck's killing spree, provided eyewitness testimony during the trial. Speck was sentenced to death. After his death sentence was deemed unconstitutional in 1972 following the Furman decision, he was resentenced to twelve hundred years in prison (Wikipedia, 2011l).

During his incarceration, Speck was not a model prisoner. He was often caught with illegal drugs or homemade moonshine. Punishment for these infractions was meaningless to him. "How am I going to get in trouble?" he said. "I'm here for 1,200 years!" (Wikipedia, 2011l).

In his only prison interview, granted to Bob Greene of the *Chicago Tribune* in 1978, Speck finally confessed to the murders. Nevertheless, Speck thought he would be released from prison "around the year 2000." He planned to open a grocery store after his release. In that interview, Speck's "final thought for the American people" was this: "Just tell 'em to keep up their hatred for me. I know it keeps up their morale. And I don't know what I'd do without it." He eventually died of a massive heart attack. He was forty-nine and had served nineteen years of his twelve-hundred-year sentence (Greene, 1983).

The ten-year national moratorium on executions ended on January 17, 1977, when Gary Mark Gilmore was executed by a firing squad in Utah. Gilmore was born into a dysfunctional family. His father was a violent alcoholic who often abused his wife and three sons. Gilmore's life of crime began when he was fourteen, and he was in and out of penitentiaries for a variety of crimes until he was conditionally paroled in 1976 (Wikipedia, 2011e; Mailer, 1979).

On July 20, 1976, Gilmore robbed and then killed motel manager Bennie Bushnell in Provo, Utah. According to testimony, Gilmore ordered Bushnell to lie down on the floor and then shot him in cold blood. Gilmore was also charged with murdering gas-station employee Max Jensen in Orem, Utah, the previous day. That case never went to trial because there were no witnesses. After a two-day trial, Gilmore was convicted of the Bushnell murder and received the death penalty. At the time, Utah had two methods of execution, hanging or death by firing squad. Gilmore said, "I'd prefer to be shot" (Wikipedia, 2011e; Mailer, 1979).

Gilmore spent three months on death row and tried to commit suicide two times. He never challenged his death sentence and, in fact, railed against those who spoke out against the death penalty and tried to save his life: "This is my life and this is my death. It's been sanctioned by the courts that I die and I accept that" (Wikipedia, 2011e; Mailer, 1979).

Gilmore was executed by firing squad on January 17, 1977, after demanding his lawyers drop the appeals they filed in defiance of his wishes. His last words were, "Let's do it." That same year, Oklahoma became the first state to adopt lethal injection for executions.

4

Cycle of Violence

In the wake of the Odle family murders, a single portrait of the family taken within a year before the murders was circulated and accompanied many of the front-page stories. Fourteen-year-old Robyn would have probably grown up to look like her mother. Robyn had her mother's dark eyes, oval face, and dark hair. They even had similar haircuts.

The two younger boys, Scott and Sean, and their father, Robert, smile for the camera. Scott has some mischief in his eyes. Robert anchors the picture with his arm around his wife, looking like "everydad." It could have been the nature of the lighting in the original print or the fact that a color photo had been transferred to a black-and-white image, but Sean's face glows brighter than the rest. He absolutely beams. His smile, his countenance, his square-shouldered posture make him stand out from the rest of his family. Nothing in his expression provides a single clue about his home life.

Carolyn stares past, almost through, the camera. Her eyes are intense. But one gets the feeling that her mind was somewhere else. The look on Tom's face, in the lower left of the picture, suggests he would rather be anywhere else than sitting for a family photo.

Despite the social restrictions his mother imposed on him, Tom clearly experienced and enjoyed some of the standard social activities of youth.

Baseball, Paper Routes, and Junior High School

Summer was always the same. I longed for the baseball season to start so I could get out of the house for a little while. By the time I was 11 years old, I had made the little league faction of the city baseball league. I was given a uniform to wear, which made me feel really big time. I was good enough to be picked for a team, and I was given an actual baseball uniform to wear. Also, I had come in second by one point in the city Cub Scout track meet. Although my dad only saw me play baseball one time, he tried to come and see me play a few other times. But the coach didn't play me because my mother had called and complained to him about me. So, he sat me on the bench a lot after that and told me that if she ever called again, I would be kicked off the team. I knew I was better than a lot of those kids on the team, but he wouldn't play me after that.

During the time I was involved in the Cub Scouts, my mother was a Den Mother. I never liked that because it was as if she became two different people. During the Scout meetings she was actually cool to be around. But when there were no kids around, she was the same old mother I was growing to despise. My grades were average, I guess, because I never really tried. I felt that no matter what I did, I could never win. So, I just did the work and that was it. However, a lot of work I never did because I rarely brought work home to do. That was the number one complaint by my teachers to my parents. They always said that I never applied myself. And if I did apply myself, I could be a straight A student. I just didn't care. At home I was isolated, because my sister and brothers were too young to play with. So, I spent a lot of time alone doing jig-saw puzzles, drawing in my room, and listening to the radio. Whenever I went into the living room to watch TV, I was told to get out.

My sixth grade year was a disaster. Me and this kid, Mark, got into about three or four fights and I got suspended a lot for the fighting. But I really didn't care. The teachers were people I didn't like at all. They used to call all the kids by their first name, except me, because there were two kids with the name Tom. So, they called me Odle and they called the other kid Tom. I asked them about it one time and was told to sit down before they called me something else. But I was also on the school patrol in the sixth grade. We stopped traffic and helped the kids cross the street. I enjoyed that because I was always pulling the Captain spot on the draw out of the hat. So, I was always in charge, it seemed. I guess I needed to feel some sort of purpose for being and that was it: Captain of the School Patrol at Horace Mann School.

My brother Sean had some sort of blood problem that caused him to go into Children's Hospital in St. Louis. During that time, one of the family members on my father's side got caught bribing my brother with some candy to tell him about my mother's treatment of the kids. This caused a huge separation in the family to a point where my cousins rarely came around the house at all because of my mother. And of course, my mother turned me against them all by telling me they were no good and filling my head with lies, or so I found out years later. So, I never really knew my uncle, aunt, cousins, nobody. They had some reports on my mom because she was always talking about how she hated my brother Sean. She got pregnant too soon after having my sister, and she had her gall bladder removed. She just used all that against Sean.

I guess when I look back on it I resented Sean, too. I resented being made to take care of him. As we got older, I vented on him somewhat because my mother made me take care of him. It wasn't his fault, but he paid for it anyway. I look back now and feel ashamed of how I treated Sean, sometimes. I was the person who took care of him most of his life. I was the person who told him to always say that I had made him do the things that would get him beaten. Yet, he took some punches and endured some wrestling matches he shouldn't have.

I loved baseball, and I used to love going to my grandparents' house to listen to the games on the radio with my grandpa. I loved that old man. And I think he loved me or at least he cared for me more than he did his own daughter, my mother. He did a lot of time in WWII, and we would talk about it sometimes. He even had some stuff from the war, and I used to love to look at it. He would let me get a beer every now and then, but not too often. We would have to sit on the back step, because my grandma allowed no smoking or beer drinking in the house. So, in the summer, he would have a cigarette and a bottle of Budweiser, and of course, I'd be right there.

Then my mother started shipping Sean to my grandparents' as often as she could, just to get rid of him. That prevented me from going out there as much as I did before. I understand now, but then I didn't understand that I hated my brother Sean for it. I really believe that my mom played me against Sean. She knew how much I loved going out to see my grandpa.

My sister and I were as far apart as two people could be. I never really felt anything for her, to be honest. I don't even know if I liked her or not. The age difference didn't help, either. It was only about five years, but at that time, it seemed like a lot of time. When we saw each other in school, we never waved or even acknowledged that we knew each other. I don't know if that's normal or not.

The concept of the "cycle of violence" is a widely accepted and frequently cited theory regarding the effects of child abuse. In "The Cycle of Violence," about the intergenerational transmission of violence, Dr. Cathy Widom reports, "Among adults who were abused as children, between one-fifth and one-third abuse their own children" (1989).

The counterpoints to such findings are that many children who have suffered abuse do not become abusers, do not manifest violent aggressive behavior later in life, do not commit criminal offenses, and do not kill their families. However, rarely are aspects of human behavior simply constituted by direct 1:1 cause-and-effect relationships. Many variables collectively define the complex matrix of human thought and behavior: genetic makeup, personality traits, moral development, neuropsychological abnormalities, psychiatric disorders, observational learning from role models, social learning, peer influences, and the selective reinforcement of specific behavioral patterns during childhood and adolescence.

At the age of eleven, Tom began to finally experience some independence from his mother.

I went on to the seventh grade and met a whole bunch of new kids. It was sort of a fresh start. I just tried to do what I could at school to be accepted by somebody. As it turned out, the kids who accepted me were the kids who smoked and did drugs. I thought they were the cool kids. We used to sneak off campus and smoke during lunch and then go back to school or ditch, if everybody was going to go.

I really liked woodshop class. I felt like I belonged in there, and I liked the teacher because he would give step-by-step instructions. He would even show us how to make something and then tell us to make it without any help. I liked that a lot because it was something I could do on my own, without someone breathing down my neck.

At about the same time, I had to start playing an instrument, the violin. My godmother played the violin in high school, so my mom made me play it. I was in the school orchestra, which was not a cool place to be, but I endured it and tried real hard. We even won some musical festival when I was in the seventh grade. I don't remember too much about it except that I was nervous and tried my best. To me, that was cool. But my mom couldn't have cared less. She shrugged it off like it was nothing. When I hit a game-winning home run in little league, I got a pizza, but nothing for that one.

I had a paper route at that time, also. I was able to buy my own television: a twelve-inch black and white. But it was mine and I paid for it. I was also able to buy a good radio and a new bike. And finally, I could do some of the things I could never do before. I would keep most of the tips and never give them to my mom to put in the bank deposit. So, I had my own walking-around money.

My mom started going out more at night around that time. I would be left in charge to babysit the siblings. I was not allowed to go out, so I would stay at home while she went out and did her running around. She was on a bowling league on some of the nights, but I really didn't care what she was doing. She was out of the house and she wasn't there. I would feel so relieved when she was not around, like a weight had been taken off me. Nothing really changed though because I was pretty much in charge of my siblings, anyway. I had to fix the meals and clean the house, pretty much like some live-in maid, or at least that's how I felt at the time.

When I got to the eighth grade, I stopped playing baseball. I had tried out for the school baseball team and I made it. But my mom told me that I had to quit, so I quit. I was too old to play little league, so there wasn't much left. I went out for track, and since the coach never cut anybody, I made the team. But I never ran a race.

My mom had a friend who had a kid my age. We would go over there a lot, so he and I became friends. We were on a young bowling league that bowled every Saturday morning. I was pretty decent and so was he. We used to compete as to who had the best series and the best game. It was cool. I used to spend the night at his house, sometimes. He lived by the mall, so we would go to the mall and hang out. I was getting some freedom for the first time and it felt good.

I had two paper routes by that time, and I was doing real well. I was mowing yards, raking leaves, shoveling snow, anything for extra money. But, I was buying record albums, playing arcade games, and not saving anything, as I really should have been doing. My dad got me a used 8-track stereo with a turntable, so I was happy and really getting into music.

I remember one time me and my friend Rod were raking leaves in his part of town and we were burning them. This other kid that he knew said he would jump over the fire for a quarter. But when he did he fell in the fire and got burned a little bit. It wasn't anything serious. He singed his hair and got some minor burns. But we got in trouble because we gave the kid a quarter for attempting to jump through the fire.

I got caught smoking by my mom at our eighth grade party, which was just before graduation. She made me smoke a whole pack of cigarettes, one right after the other, until I was sick.

At about that same time, I got jumped by some black kids because I wouldn't let them take my bike from me. I got beat up pretty bad, but I still had my bike when it was all said and done. Afterwards, I felt that they jumped me because I was white. And I still believe that I was introduced to racism that day. I never knew what racism was up until then. At the time, it seemed like they expected me to give them my bike because they believed that they deserved it. I never told anyone I got beat up by black people. I always said I fell off my bike doing a jump. I didn't want to make a bad situation worse and cause even more trouble at school. From then on, I had a bad opinion about black people. I didn't hate them, but I didn't want anything to do with them. I always thought of getting some sort of revenge on them for beating me up. But I never did.

I did O.K. in junior high school. I started finding out about sex a little bit: just some touching and kissing, and not much more than that. My grades were the same as always: average without even trying. I kick myself now for not applying myself, because I think I could have become anything

I set my sights on being. I just couldn't get past the lack of recognition or approval from my parents. I wanted so badly for my mom's approval and I never got it. I never heard her say she loved me, except once after a beating when I was 5. I never heard her say that she was proud of me. I never heard my father say those things, either.

I don't know what it was about her, but she did not seem to be able to say anything favorable. I know she was raised in a somewhat similar situation in which there was hardly any emotion shown, but damn, did she have to ruin my emotional state, also? All of us were screwed up when I look back on how things were at home.

Adolescent Aggression and Predictors of Violence

Genetically, Tom Odle was the offspring of an overcontrolled, defensive, and emotionally detached woman of rigid character and an affable but passive and submissive man. Tom manifested early aggressive tendencies as demonstrated by frequent fighting at school and physically abusing his brother Sean. Tom's aggressive tendencies were acquired, in part, as a result of experiential learning (i.e., experiencing his mother's repeated physical abuse), observational learning (i.e., watching his mother abuse his brother), and social reinforcement (e.g., increased attention from classmates). Although he manifested no significant or disabling neuropsychological impairment, he appears to have manifested depression beginning in early adolescence, characterized by social alienation, poor motivation, and self-medication via substance abuse.

From the ages of ten to fifteen, Tom's behavior began to reveal the classic features of a burgeoning conduct disorder. Fighting became commonplace, and he was expelled from school as a result. The resentment he held for his mother was displaced to his younger brother, and in the perversely cruel dynamics of intrafamilial abuse, his abuse of his brother was encouraged and reinforced by his mother. Promiscuous sex, drug abuse, and property crime, other classic features of adolescent conduct disorder, appeared as well. Although it is easy to take the view that such behaviors simply reflect the natural evolution of a bad child, it is also important and meaningful to consider the factors that shape and reinforce maladaptive behavior during adolescence.

An exhaustive analysis of predictors of violence during adolescence was conducted by the Office of Juvenile Justice and Delinquency Prevention, U.S. Department of Justice (Hawkins et al., 2000). A meta-analysis of sixty-six empirical studies that examined various factors found to be predictive of violence reveal at least twenty-seven predictors from five different domains, including individual factors, family factors, school factors, peer-related factors, and community/neighborhood factors (see table 1). Tom manifested at least ten of these twenty-seven factors during childhood.

Table 1. Predictors of youth violence

Individual factors
    Pregnancy and delivery complications
    Low resting heart rate
    Internalizing disorders
    Hyperactivity, attention/concentration problems,
       restlessness, and risk taking
    Aggressiveness
    Early initiation of violent behavior
    Involvement in other forms of antisocial behavior
    Beliefs and attitudes favorable to deviant or antisocial behavior

Family factors
    Parental criminality
    Child maltreatment
    Poor family-management practices
    Low levels of parental involvement
    Poor family bonding; family conflict
    Parental attitudes favorable to substance use and violence
    Parent-child separation

School factors
    Academic failure
    Low bonding to school
    Truancy and dropping out of school
    Frequent school transitions

Peer-related factors
    Delinquent siblings
    Delinquent peers
    Gang membership

Community and neighborhood factors
    Poverty
    Community disorganization
    Availability of drugs and firearms
    Neighborhood adults involved in crime
    Exposure to violence and racial prejudice

SOURCE: Adapted from "Predictors of Youth Violence," by J. D. Hawkins, T. I. Herrenkohl, D. P. Farrington, D. Brewer, R. F. Catalona, T. W. Harachi, and L. Cothern, 2000, *Juvenile Justice Bulletin*, Office of Juvenile Justice and Delinquency Prevention, U.S. Department of Justice, pp. 1–11.

John Wayne Gacy; the Ford Heights Four

John Wayne Gacy was born on March 17, 1942. His loving mother kept a clean and tidy house, and his sisters doted on him. But his father was a mean drunk who periodically unleashed his anger on his family with beatings and other forms of physical abuse. Nevertheless, Gacy loved his father very much and longed for his acceptance. Gacy was hungry for praise and approval and felt he never lived up to his father's expectations. Gacy did not graduate high school but did graduate from Northwestern Business College (Wikipedia, 2011g).

In December 1978 in Des Plaines, Illinois, Gacy was arrested and eventually charged with the rapes and murders of thirty-three teenage boys (as young as fourteen years old) and young men. Gacy buried the bodies of twenty-six of them in the crawl space underneath his house until he ran out of room and then started putting them, three in all, in his backyard. He dumped the last four in the nearby Des Plaines River, Gacy said, because there was no room at his house. Some of the victim's bodies were so badly decomposed they were never identified (Wikipedia, 2011g).

His trial began thirteen months later. The main point of contention during the trial was whether or not Gacy was insane at the time he committed all of the murders. However, given the overwhelming evidence against him, he was ultimately convicted of the thirty-three murders. Following his conviction, the state asked that Gacy be given the death penalty for the twelve murders known to have occurred since the Illinois statute of capital punishment became effective in 1977. On March 13, 1980, following a highly publicized trial that drew massive media attention, Gacy was sentenced to death. He spent fourteen years on death row at the Menard Correctional Center in Illinois before the appeals process ran its course.

At age fourteen, Tom Odle watched the reports of the heinous murders and the announcement of Gacy's death sentence on the evening news. Little did he know that one day he, too, would be confronted by Gacy and be forced to deal with Gacy's sadistic homosexual urges. However, when that day came, unlike the thirty-three victims who suffered and died as a result of Gacy's psychopathic homicidal tendencies, Tom was aware that his death-row neighbor was a serial sex killer and a monster. Enraged and disgusted by Gacy's advances, Tom proceeded to punch him out.

During the same time that young Tom watched the news reports of the Gacy murders, an unrelated crime occurred that would ultimately change his life. In 1978, a double murder was committed in Chicago that the media labeled the Ford Heights Four case. Verneal Jimerson and Dennis Williams were eventually convicted of the crime and sentenced to death. Two other men were also convicted in relation to the crime but did not receive death sentences. Based on evidence developed by Rob Warden of the *Chicago Lawyer* and investigative journalism students at Northwestern University under the direction of professor David Protess that included witness coercion, perjury, false forensic testimony, and prosecutorial misconduct, Jimerson and Williams were exonerated in the summer of 1996. The civil lawsuits that followed included such strong evidence of official misconduct by the police and prosecutors involved in the case that Cook County opted to settle by paying the Ford Heights Four $36 million (Center for Wrongful Convictions, 2011).

5

"I Was Doing Really Well"

By the early 1980s, America's youth culture was being driven by a relatively new art form: music videos. When MTV took to the airwaves in 1979, new stars were born. They were fashion icons as well as rock stars, and they could sell a million T-shirts or pairs of shoes—as well as records—with a single close-up.

One of the cultural phenomena of MTV was that media saturation made mainstream that which once seemed revolutionary. But after running the same three to four minutes on the air a few thousand times, even the most breakthrough new look got old, or worse, tired. Hair got longer, and nobody cared. Clothes got tighter, shorter, and ripped to shreds, and television's ability to serve it up en masse made it all seem less outrageous than it would have once been. With each new production, the video stars tried to visually outdo one another. But through incessant repetition, the medium put all of that outrageousness into a blender and homogenized it. And what once was edgy became soft and safe.

Tom Odle's band preferences (guitar bands more than video stars) indicate he was more concerned with the music than with being a fashionista. But the look he adopted—that of the long-haired, flannel-shirted, concert-T crowd—would have commanded more attention from parents, teachers, and administrators just a few years earlier. Tom and his friends may have felt like they were rebelling, but they no longer looked as rebellious. Had he looked more like he felt, someone may have tried a little harder to intervene in Tom's life.

Sex, Drugs, and Early Criminal Behavior

I graduated junior high school without any problems. I was thirteen years old entering high school. Because my birthday is in December, I was always the youngest in my class. High school was different. Rod and I were still friends, and we continued doing the bowling thing. My mom and I went to a bowling tournament once, but that was as far as it went. It was fun though, because I got a city trophy out of it for winning the city mixed doubles. I was still watching my brothers and sister as the built-in babysitter.

That year I met another guy who would later turn out to play a part in my life that screwed things up. I had continued smoking, despite the incident in which I got sick after being forced to smoke a whole pack of cigarettes. I just had to be cool like all the other kids who hung out on the smoker's corner: the long haired kids with the jeans, flannel shirts, concert jerseys, and cigarettes hanging out of their mouths. I was getting out a little more, but not like I wanted. When I was supposed to be watching the siblings, I was sneaking out of the house and doing other things like going to parties, which is when I started to drink and do drugs.

I first started smoking reefer when I was a freshman in high school, about thirteen years old. I didn't do it too much at first, but as time went on and I enjoyed the feeling, I really got into it. But I never did it at school. Not yet, anyway. I would smoke cigarettes, but that was it. I changed my dress to match that of the cool kids. I finally even convinced my dad to stop cutting my hair, so it started to grow out. My grades were never of any interest, and I was always able to float by with the exception of English class. I hated that class. I could never understand all the diagramming of sentences. So I failed the class and had to make it up during summer school.

I was introduced to sex when I turned fourteen. I was a freshman in high school and still had my paper routes. One day, I was collecting for the month, and this one woman asked me to come into her bedroom because she said that's where she kept her purse. Her name was Linda, and she was a long-legged blonde. She was only wearing a robe, and it came open in the front, or she let it come open. I don't know which and I didn't care. I was just looking at her exposed breasts. When she saw that I was looking, she asked if I wanted to see more and touch them. Of course, I did. From there, she asked if I wanted to see more and touch more. Then she asked if I knew how to have sex, and I told her I was a virgin. From there, she more or less taught me everything there was to know about sex. And of course, she was the last stop on my paper route every single night. I thought it was great, and I wanted to do it all the time. I even started having sex with her during lunchtime.

I never figured out why she did what she did. I didn't know if she was doing me a favor by teaching me the ins and outs of sex, or if she was lonely and looking for some affection like I was, or if she was molesting me. Guys don't complain when they're having sex at that age, especially with a woman who is twenty-eight. She was fine, too. And it lasted for several years, even after I was fired from my paper routes. I was fired because people were complaining that I was getting later and later with deliveries, because of the time I was spending with Linda. I also had broken a few doors, so the newspaper felt it was time for me to move on and I was fired. Linda and I carried on our sexual encounters anywhere and everywhere possible. I would even skip school and she would call in my excuse as to why I was absent.

At about that time, I was introduced to drafting at school. I really enjoyed that class. I had taken a general shop course for freshmen, and part of that class involved drafting. I have always loved building things and being creative with my hands. I found the drafting class to be the perfect opportunity and decided that I wanted to be an architect. I had finally found something in school that really interested me besides hanging around with cool kids and trying to be like them. I did my very best, which was O.K., nothing spectacular. But I enjoyed it very much. I also enjoyed the wood shop classes. It was my thing, so to speak. I thought that I had finally found where I belonged.

One time, we had a project in drafting class which involved designing a home. I had done research on the project, and even my mom helped me get some of the materials I needed. I really thought I had laid out this home so perfectly and that everybody would have no choice but to recognize me for my skill and be proud of me. The day came and I made an "A" on it. Nothing was wrong with my draft, and the teacher wanted to put it and a few others on display in the school. But then, I showed it to my mother. All she could say was "is that the best you can do? It looks like garbage." I was crushed. I was devastated by her reaction and from then on, I didn't care about drafting. In fact, I stopped going to drafting and eventually I quit the class. Instead, I just hung with the wood shop classes and made things for my grandma and grandpa. To this day, every time I try and draw a house or draft a house plan, I hear those words echoing in my head: "it looks like garbage." Those words won't go away. Afterwards, I started getting high in school, and my attitude was that I just didn't care at all.

I really believe that my mother was crazy, because that would excuse a lot of the things she did. But there were times when she was the coolest mom around. She knew every band I liked, and if there was a sale on albums or tapes, she would get them for me. She always made sure I had the coolest concert jerseys and stuff like that. It was almost like she was two different people.

I was still seeing Linda, regularly, during the rest of my freshman year. And, I started dating some girls from school, but just to get sex. If I didn't get it, then I would leave them and move on to the next one. My summer was not good. I had met this girl in my civics class, and we started dating during the summer. I really liked her, but she was a year older than me. Anyway, she and I started hanging out over the summer and things were really cool. I thought I had finally met a girl I could hang out with. We dated, but we never had sex. We always went to the park and walked around, talked, and just hung out.

Then one day, this guy with whom I had gotten into a fight at school saw us at the park. He was with his friends and they jumped me in front of her and beat me up, pretty bad. There were several of them, so I had no chance of defending myself, whatsoever. But the worst thing was that I got beat up in front of a girl I really liked. When my dad found out about it, he went to the police to press charges. At that point, she found out that I was only fourteen, instead of fifteen like she thought. So, that was the end of that relationship before it really got started. She wouldn't even talk to me after that. I didn't want my dad to press charges because I would have to go back to school and face those guys again. And, not only that, but I would have a bad reputation for being somebody who runs to the police and that's not cool for a kid, at all. But it was out of my hands and he did it.

Rod had moved over the summer, so I started hanging out with this guy Glen, who used to stay at the house behind ours. Glen and I hung out for the rest of that summer, getting high, drinking, and chasing girls. He was older than me by a couple of years. He would be a senior when I was a sophomore. I got braces that summer, also. So, I had a mouth full of metal and an "I don't care" attitude. Needless to say, I got into a few more fights that I wished I had avoided. Those braces would really cut up my mouth.

By the time my sophomore year came along, I was finally cool. I had long hair. I smoked cigarettes and I got high at school. I was even hanging with the older crowd, mainly seniors. Things were pretty good. But I wasn't paying any attention in school. I used to walk Tanya home from school and then hang at her place for a while because I didn't want to go home. I had always liked Tanya and I told her mom I liked her. Her mom always liked me and she knew what my background was like, meaning my mom and the situation at home. Her mom always used to tell me that I should let Tanya know how I really felt about her. But I was too shy to come on that strong with her. I guess I liked her too much. I found out later that she really liked me too. But nothing ever came of it. We were just friends and had known each other for years.

Then, this kid, Brad, moved in up the street from me. So, I got to know him and we started getting high and drunk. He was just someone close by to party with. He was in my math class first thing in the morning, so we'd get high before school and go to math class. I made straight A's in math class, surprisingly enough. Nothing much happened during that school year, except the neighbors down the street started blaming me for everything that happened to them. They called the police on several occasions, but nobody ever found out what was going on, and they eventually moved away. But it was really weird. They kept blaming me for things I didn't do. I was too busy getting high. I was also learning how to break into houses at that time. But I wasn't breaking into the houses in my own neighborhood.

Halfway through my sophomore year, I got my driver's permit. But my dad was the only one who would take me out driving. I used to drive my dad around everywhere he needed to go. My mom never took me out driving. And she only rode in the car while I was driving one time, and only because she had to. I used to ask my mom if I could drive, and she would always say "no." It felt good to be able to drive because I felt like I was getting older and closer to getting out of the house. However, my parents did not want me to work while I was in school because they thought it would inter-fere with my schoolwork. I should have told them that I was maintaining a "C" average without doing any schoolwork at all. The only work I was able to do after I got fired from my paper routes was mowing yards during the summer, raking leaves in the fall, and shoveling snow during the winter.

When summer came after my sophomore year, all hell broke loose. I was introduced to the world of real drugs, like LSD, cocaine, dust, and heroin. I was also made aware of the money that could be made selling reefer and breaking into peoples' houses. Glen and I used to break into houses, wipe them out, sell the stuff, and go get high. I even made it into a business. People would tell me what they were looking for, and when I broke into a house, I would look for those items. I only took what I could find quickly, whereas Glen would take everything that wasn't nailed down. My dad had given me a portable police scanner that I could carry with me. So, I would know if the police were called or if they were on their way. I would get rid of my stuff right away, but Glen would be left trying to sell his stuff to anybody who would buy it.

Conduct Disorder

Tom Odle's drug abuse escalated relatively quickly from age thirteen to sixteen, and his engagement in property crime, including burglary and theft as well as drug sales, increased as a function of his drug abuse. His early marijuana and alcohol abuse provided him with an escape hatch from his problems at home, a distraction from his negative self-image, and acceptance by selective subgroups of his peers: the partiers and the dopers. As such, there were multiple reinforcers for his growing drug abuse. But drugs aren't cheap, and the money earned from paper routes and mowing yards won't support a growing drug habit. As a result, Tom quickly learned that selling stolen goods from homes that he burglarized and selling drugs were far more profitable than the legitimate jobs he had done earlier. But the increasing variety and frequency of his criminal endeavors were driven by more than just money. In his underdeveloped adolescent sense of self, which had been irreparably damaged by the psychological abuse he had sustained and continued to sustain from his mother, the attention he received from his peers as a result of his status as a drug dealer and rebel was invaluable.

Clinically, from the age of fourteen to sixteen, Tom manifested a full-blown conduct disorder. The diagnostic criteria for conduct disorder are presented in table 2. He engaged in frequent fights with his peers and was periodically truant from school. The frequency and variety of his drug abuse escalated. His criminal activities expanded from shoplifting and petty theft to burglary, auto theft, and drug sales. As a result of the drugs and money that he had at that time, he finally received the attention from his peers that had previously eluded him.

However, despite his expanding criminal repertoire during this stage of adolescence, he was yet to commit a violent criminal act. Nevertheless, this key stage of personality development was characterized by the appearance of numerous antisocial tendencies and behaviors that would increase in frequency and intensity as he continued to mature, due in part to the reinforcement he received, including money, sex, and attention from his peers. Although his self-concept was bolstered by the reinforcement he received from his friends, this period represents the beginning of the downward spiral of psychological dissolution that would end with the horrific crime that he was to commit two years later.

> I was doing really well. I was able to do a few things for
> Linda, and we went out on the town a few times. And of
> course, Linda and I were still going at it. I was going to con-
> certs in rented limos and buying tickets, drugs, and alcohol
> for my friends. I was living good for the moment. I was buy-
> ing nice clothes with cash. I was O.K. and finally feeling like
> I was accepted, liked, and even loved. Because I had cocaine,
> there were some fine women hanging around all the time.
> They would do anything for that cocaine. Now I know it was

all about the cocaine, but you couldn't have told me that back then. I would have sworn they were loving me and doing things because they loved me.

　　I met this one girl Denise over the summer though, who was pretty decent. She really wasn't into the drug scene, but she was into the music scene, like I was. We started going out just before my junior year started. But that was right about the time Glen got arrested for trying to sell some of the stolen merchandise to an undercover cop. Of course, my name came up, and they came and arrested me, too. But since I

Table 2. Diagnostic criteria for conduct disorder

A. A repetitive and persistent pattern of behavior in which the basic rights of others or major age-appropriate societal norms or rules are violated, as manifested by the presence of three (or more) of the following criteria in the past twelve months, with at least one criterion present in the past six months:

Aggression to people and animals
    1. Often bullies, threatens, or intimidates others
    2. Often initiates physical fights
    3. Has used a weapon that can cause serious physical harm to others
    4. Has been physically cruel to people
    5. Has been physically cruel to animals
    6. Has stolen while confronting a victim
    7. Has forced someone into sexual activity

Destruction of property
    8. Has deliberately engaged in fire setting with the intention of causing serious damage
    9. Has deliberately destroyed others' property

Deceitfulness or theft
    10. Has broken into someone else's house, building, or car
    11. Often lies to obtain goods or favors or to avoid obligations
    12. Has stolen items of nontrivial value without confronting a victim

Serious violations of rules
    13. Often stays out at night despite parental prohibitions, beginning before age thirteen
    14. Has run away from home overnight at least twice
    15. Is often truant from school, beginning before age thirteen

B. The disturbance in behavior causes clinically significant impairment in social, academic, or occupational functioning

C. If the individual is age eighteen years or older, criteria are not met for antisocial personality disorder

SOURCE: Adapted from *Diagnostic and statistical manual of mental disorders*, American Psychiatric Association, 2000, Washington, DC: APA, pp. 93–99.

was underage, I was released to my parents. Glen was sent to jail. They only got me for some of the things I had done. I had stolen cars from car lots and a few motorcycles. You name it, I had taken it. My parents lost all trust in me, and I don't blame them. I really shamed them, although I didn't care what my mother thought. I only cared that I shamed my father because I had sold some stolen lawnmower equipment to one of his friends. My father made me tell his friend what I had done to his face and give him his money back. I did it because I owed my dad that much respect. Don't ask me why. It was just something I felt I had to do. Brad got called in also because his dad found a riding lawn mower at his house and called the police about it. I took the weight for it even though Brad stole it. Brad had originally brought it to my house, but I couldn't hold it there without raising suspicion.

Denise and I were dating at that time, but no sex yet, because she wanted to wait until she was ready, and I respected that. I really liked her a lot. My dad was going to give me his car when I turned sixteen, but that was blown after I got arrested. I really doubt my mother would have let that take place, anyway. I had to go through a lot of stuff to rebuild the trust my father had in me. But my mother was still going out all the time, and I was sneaking off at night, just making it back before she came home. I was still doing a little stealing too, but just enough to stay high most of the time. I was smoking reefer and doing cocaine and some heroin. I would do the other stuff when it was around, but it wasn't as abundant as the stuff I was doing. The whole time Linda thought I was going to jail. So, any time I wasn't out getting high or with Denise, I was with Linda.

I had to go through a lot of court dates, but I finally had this deal worked out through my public defender. I had to do a week in a detention center, and then I had to complete a UDIS [Unified Delinquency Intervention Services] program where my old math teacher was my sponsor. I also got two years of probation and a three hundred dollar fine to replace the windows and doors I had damaged going into the houses. I had to work to pay the fine off, and part of that was to wash the vehicles where my dad worked. So, all the Illinois Bell cars, trucks, and vans were being washed by me, once a month. That was part of the punishment given to me by my father for the burglaries. I worked there for about three months or so, until I wrecked a van after washing it. I backed it into a truck. That caused me to be let go. For Christmas that year, my father paid off the remaining debt I had owed because he knew if I was left to pay it off, I would have resorted to my old habits. I don't know about my father and me. I was really angry with him for all the things he allowed my mother to do to me, but yet I really liked my dad, and I didn't want to put him through anything he didn't need to go through. I also felt sorry for him, because he was a good guy. He just wouldn't stand up to my mother.

My crime partner, Glen, got some time in prison, like five or six years. I'm not sure exactly how much. I got lucky with my part in that whole thing. And not only was I lucky with the sentence, I made more money than he did, and I had a better time than he did. I look back now and wonder where my head was at, because I could have done so much better with that time, instead of spending it the way I did. I hurt so many people and destroyed my father's faith in me, if he ever had any to begin with.

My mother only came one time to a court hearing. And she actually told the judge to lock me up and throw away the key because she never wanted me anyway. My father gave her a look I will never forget, but he said nothing to her. I had even tried to rebuild something with my mother, if there ever was anything to rebuild, by helping her out with her PTO nights at Horace Mann School. I would work a few of the games and help out when I could. But I don't know if it helped or hurt.

My UDIS sponsor and I got along great. He was into computers and got me into computers. I was able to buy my own computer, a Commodore VIC 20. During our sessions we would work with the computer, finding out all the possibilities it had. We interfaced with it and enjoyed music at the same time. He was one of those hippie guys from the 60s, so he and his wife were people after my own soul. I really took off with the computer and was trying to write my own programs. I never told anyone what I was doing because I didn't want to hear about how huge a failure I was. But my sponsor was supportive of my endeavors and helped me out.

When we were through with the UDIS program, he gave me this old Honda 50 motorcycle that was not running. I was able to get it up and going and had some fun with it before I had to get rid of it. I was out riding it and was trying to show off in front of some girls. But the clutch grabbed on me, and the bike took off and hit a girl's bike while she was sitting on it. She called the police because the motorcycle had bent her front wheel. So I got three tickets that night for trying to impress some girls. I got tickets for improper classification, illegal U-turn, and leaving the scene of an accident. Needless to say, my mom came home while I was sitting in the back of the police car, and she told the cop to put me in jail because she was tired of dealing with me. But the cop wouldn't do it. When I went to court, I was only charged with improper classification and fined one hundred dollars.

Denise and I broke up shortly after I was sentenced. I broke up with her for some reason, which I thought, was fantastic at the time, but was really stupid. I broke up with her before she could break up with me. I mean, I wonder what I was thinking back then. She was a good girl, and I had a lot of fun with her. We never argued or fought about anything. But I had this stupid idea that I should break up with her first. Of course, I ran to Linda for comfort. That woman taught me everything I knew about sex. I just couldn't get enough of it. Now, I think that I substituted that sex with Linda for some sort of acknowledgment and acceptance that I wasn't getting anywhere else. I would have probably married her if it had been that type of thing. She was my buddy, as well as my teacher, lover, and freak. But the age gap and the situation were just too much, I guess.

About that time, a girl I had briefly dated before had been removed from her home because her stepfather was allegedly abusing her, sexually. I was asked if I had known about it, and she had told me about it, but I had done nothing about it. I guess I thought as long as she was sexing me, it was cool. She was thirteen when I was fifteen, and I had to go to trial about it, against her stepfather. The prosecutor I helped was the same one that came after me in my own trial, later. How ironic.

When I turned sixteen, I had to go spend the Christmas holiday locked in the detention center for one week to fulfill my sentence. That was something I always said I would never do again. I swore I would never come back to a place like that. I was not allowed to get my driver's license until about a week before my permit expired. If I hadn't gotten it then, I would have had to buy the permit again. Once I got my license, I had to turn it over to my dad who held on to it for what seemed like forever. I really wanted that license bad because it was like a rite of passage, and it was being held from me. But it was being held from me because of the crimes I had committed. I was being punished. I look back now and that wasn't so bad compared to what I could have ended up with. But when you're sixteen years old, nothing is more important than those rites of passage.

I wasn't working at that time. I had done some work at a body shop for some of my father's friends. But that didn't last, as I was too lazy about sanding down the cars. I wanted to do all the other stuff, but not the sanding. So, I was let go and moved on to other things like selling reefer and stealing a few odds and ends to keep myself high. I had told myself I would never do anything to go back to that detention center. But I was stealing, doing drugs, and selling drugs again: everything that could send me back to the center.

I also started going back into houses again to get the big money, except this time I was going by myself. This way, I could only blame myself should something go wrong. I was stealing cars off the car lots, again. But the lure of the big money from the houses was something to me. I loved having that money and the attention it brought me. I loved being able to buy concert tickets for me and a few other people, and renting a limo to take us and bring us back. It was just a sense of power, maybe, or the need to please. I was enjoying myself and enjoying that everyone would have a good time. I liked that feeling. I also loved being high and away from the house.

I wasn't allowed to quit school, so I did some ditching. One of my friends lived right across the street from the high school, of all places. I would talk people into skipping with me, just to go to a different town, bum around, and maybe go shopping and eat at a pretty good place. I loved being able to afford new jewelry and clothes.

When I was at home, all I did was eat and listen to the stereo. Music really helped me through a lot of times. I would daydream as if I were the reason the song was written and as if I was living it. Music has always been my means of escape. Even today, I can put on the headphones and go back in time to when I knew things were real. I listen to everything from hard rock, heavy metal, blues, jazz, soul, and some country from the old days. There is so much emotion in music that it helps me express what I cannot at times. I used to make my parents and even my girlfriends so angry because I would be asked what was on my mind or something and I wouldn't talk. I would not talk because I didn't feel comfortable talking about me so much. I still have that problem today, so I have been told. I lived so isolated that talking was never one of my strong points.

Things were getting too hot around town, so I slowed down my breaking into houses. Plus, there were too many new people asking me to get things for them, which made me very uneasy about the whole thing. And it was bothering me about getting caught and having to face my dad again: not the fear of violence, but just the look on his face would have been too much for me. That had bothered me a lot since the first time I got caught. But, then I got caught having a party in my room. I think there were about two cases of beer in there with only a handful of people. That caused some more trouble, but I really didn't care. As a result, my dad postponed getting my car insurance, so I couldn't drive the car.

I started dating another girl at that time. We were pretty cool, I guess. We went out for several months. She was coming over and spending the nights. She would sneak out of her house at night and come over to my house. We would spend the night together about twice a week, sometimes more, sometimes less. But her father got upset and called my dad one morning because they had found her diary where she had written everything down we had done. So, needless to say, her father came unglued, and since I wasn't there, he told my dad about it. My dad didn't say anything too much about it. He just told me that he hoped I was using protection, which I wasn't. I just never did for some reason. So, she kept coming over at night, until she came too early one night and my dad caught her running behind the house. He didn't know what was going on, so he called the police and they came and picked her up. That was the end of things for us because her parents didn't want her to see me anymore.

My brother Sean began his crime spree at about that time. He started shoplifting at the local neighborhood grocery store, as I had done. I didn't discourage him, although now I know I should have. I didn't encourage him either. But still, I should have done something more positive. He was slick, though. I don't know how he stole some of the things he did, but he did it, and I was always the one he showed his loot to. Maybe he was looking for the same thing I was looking for from my mother; approval and an "I'm proud of you" statement. He would steal from many different stores, and when he got caught, he would always say what I had taught him to say when he was younger: that I told him to do it. So, of course, I would get punished too.

And he continued to have the problem of getting up at night and "stealing food," as my mother called it. So, she would lock up the cabinets and the fridge. And, since chaining me up to the bed had worked so well, she started chaining him to his bed every night at bedtime. But I got some pliers and fixed the chain so it could be undone should something happen where he would need to get out of the house, such as a fire. He was also given a bucket to use as a toilet and was chained all night long until breakfast. Of course, my father let this all happen and did nothing about it. Sean would take food at school, also. I never really got him, or I should say, I never understood why he was always taking food. He would even take the lunches that belonged to other students and some of the teachers, too.

Sean Odle and DCFS

As Sean grew up, the resentment that his mother felt for the son she never wanted was manifested in a form of child abuse that is often difficult for teachers and other people outside the home to observe in order to report it. According to multiple sources, including Sean, Tom, the teachers and principal at Horace Mann Elementary School, and eventually the Department of Children and Family Services (DCFS), Sean was frequently deprived of food in the home to punish him for violations of the code of conduct laid down by his mother. Sean would often complain of hunger while at school and was frequently accused of stealing other children's lunches. His mother would padlock the kitchen cabinets shut and chain the refrigerator door closed in the evening so he was unable to access food in the house. She often did this after he had been deprived of dinner with the rest of the family. And, before his mother left to go bowling in the evening, which she did several times a week, she would chain him to his bed, so he would be unable to leave the house to get food (J. Clemens, M. Long, and S. Milliner, personal communication, June 16, 2006; *People of the State of Illinois vs. Thomas Odle*, 1986).

Margie Long, a teacher at Horace Mann Elementary School, became increasingly concerned about Sean and suspected that he was being abused at home: "I'd gone up to the hills and brought back a box of rocks. I asked the kids to adopt a rock and make it their pet rock. And every day they kept a journal of the adventures of this rock. Sean's was a very disturbing journal, talking about how he was hungry but they had padlocked the cabinet doors, so when mommy went bowling the cabinet doors were locked. And to keep him from going out in the neighborhood, he was padlocked to the bedpost. We got so concerned at school that Jerry [Clemens, principal] made arrangements with the cafeteria for Sean to have a free breakfast every morning. You would have thought Jerry had committed a heinous crime, because mother [Carolyn] came to school. She claimed that Sean was an over-eater. Sean was a small child, and lots of times prior to Jerry arranging this with the cafeteria, we would be getting ready to go to lunch, and one of our students would say, 'My lunch is gone.' And, it would turn out, that Sean had eaten this child's lunch, stolen it out of the locker. He was not a well-fed child" (personal communication, June 16, 2006).

In response to growing concern regarding Sean's welfare, principal Clemens asked Bob Odle to come in to discuss Sean's condition. Mr. Odle denied that there were any issues with Sean at home. As a result, Clemens asked Odle to wait in an adjoining room, within earshot, while he questioned Sean about his hunger, food deprivation, and the padlocking of the cabinets by his mother. Despite hearing his son confirm the allegations, Bob continued to adamantly deny that such abuse was occurring in his home. Dismayed by the father's denial, the principal advised him to get a grip on the situation and address the problem, or he and the teachers would register a complaint with the authorities (J. Clemens, personal communication, June 16, 2006).

Shortly thereafter, events transpired that compelled Long to contact the authorities: "It was not uncommon for Sean to come to school with a black eye or some other bruises, and finally he came to school with a handful of black pills, and they were not aspirin or Tylenol. There was nothing written on them. This was the final straw in a series of Sean-related abuses. I called the Department of Children and Family Services, and they took Sean out of the home that day in late October" (personal communication, June 16, 2006).

The DCFS investigated the Odle family in response to claims of abuse and neglect. The investigation determined that Sean Odle was being tied or chained to his bed every night from 8:30 P.M. to 7:30 A.M. The practice of tethering Sean to his bed at night was reportedly initiated by his mother to prevent him from taking food from the kitchen cabinets and refrigerator. It was also reported that he was periodically deprived of meals in order to punish him for stealing food. The Odle children were often left alone in the evening while the father was at work. Mrs. Odle was frequently gone, and she would commonly leave Tom in charge of the younger children. DCFS investigators determined that Sean was being physically abused by his parents as well as his brother Tom. At that time, examination of Sean revealed multiple bruises that the boy claimed his brother inflicted. Due to these issues and concern for the boy's health and safety, combined with Mrs. Odle's resistance to DCFS interventions, Sean eventually received temporary foster home placement (*People of the State of Illinois vs. Thomas Odle*, 1986).

After notifying the parents, a representative from DCFS, accompanied by a police officer, arrived at the school to take temporary custody of Sean. According to Clemens, when Carolyn Odle arrived at the principal's office, "she was told what was going to happen. She left the office, never even looked at the boy, never even looked at him, and walked out the door. It was almost like he wasn't even there. She simply left the office, and not once did she acknowledge that Sean was there" (personal communication, June 16, 2006).

Twenty years later, Clemens reflected on Carolyn Odle's character: "Much of what Carolyn did was to build herself up. She did it well, from that perspective. She played the game. She exhibited an attitude of 'I'm in favor of doing the right thing for the kids.' I suppose I was a little bit suspicious. She wasn't your typical housewife . . . or your typical parent. You never felt like you could have a conversation with her where everything was registering. What really sticks in my mind is having your child taken out of your home and you simply walk out, accept it without any argument or discussion, just OK, walk out with the kid sitting there without exhibiting any kind of emotion. That's what is stuck in my head. Complete lack of emotional contact and she was that way with everybody. That is what I saw that day. I couldn't imagine it. I've had people want to kill me over their kids. But that's the first time I ever saw a mother completely emotionally detached from what was going on" (personal communication, June 16, 2006).

Three months after DCFS removed Sean from the Odle home, Long was scheduled to testify in a hearing regarding the matter: "In January, there was a hearing at the courthouse where the parents would go and petition to get Sean back into the home. And I remember so well the day. . . . I was home on sick leave because I had surgery. . . . They were going to call me from the courthouse when it was time for me to come and testify. They called and said there is no need to come. The parents didn't show" (personal communication, June 16, 2006).

> DCFS was involved with our family pretty deep by that time, also. My parents had been going through some sort of counseling, due to the chaining of my brother to the bed and him taking food at school. I think there were also some bruises where he and I had been wrestling pretty out of control. They had taken my brother out of the home for several months and put him with a foster family. I really had no feelings about it because I had the room to myself from then on. DCFS had been involved with our family for many years prior to them placing Sean in the foster home. People had been complaining about my brother at school, and he had been telling people he was being chained to his bed at night. So, they came and investigated and took him away.

Carolyn reportedly insisted that Sean's behavior was the fundamental problem and that counseling focused on her parenting skills was unnecessary and misdirected. The case was closed in February 1985. Sean was eventually returned to the Odle home. Why DCFS returned Sean to the Odle home and closed the case remains unclear. Bob and Carolyn reluctantly underwent a program of counseling with DCFS caseworkers, despite Carolyn's opposition to such intervention. Apparently, the permanency goal of DCFS in the Odle case was reunification of the family. DCFS achieved its goal by reuniting Sean with his family. However, if Sean had been allowed to remain in foster care, instead of being returned to the Odle home, he would likely be alive today. Conversely, it is clear that DCFS did not intervene on Tom's behalf because no one, including Tom, ever reported that he was abused until several years later. If DCFS had removed Tom from the Odle home because of the abuse he suffered or because of the abuse he inflicted on Sean, the murders of the Odle family members may have been prevented.

During Tom's capital murder trial, Larry Johnson, a DCFS supervisor, testified that his office's investigation of the Odle family revealed that Sean had suffered significant abuse: "It was a physical abuse situation. There were two different perpetrators, both the parents and the brother. It was a situation in which Sean was abused over two different periods of time by the parents and one period of time by the brother that was substantiated." As a result, he noted that Sean was placed in a foster home for a period of time and subsequently returned to the Odle home, following a program of counseling with Mr. and Mrs. Odle, which was focused on correcting their parenting techniques. When questioned with regard to the claims of abuse of Tom, Johnson noted that Sean informed his foster mother that Tom had also been chained to his bed, several years earlier, in a manner similar to that used with Sean (*People of the State of Illinois vs. Thomas Odle*, 1986).

Lethal Injection

In 1977, Oklahoma became the first state to adopt lethal injection as a means of execution. That was the same year Gary Gilmore was executed by a firing squad in Utah. Lethal injection was adopted to replace other forms of execution that were considered less humane: electrocution, hanging, the gas chamber, and the firing squad. It was five more years until Charles Brooks Jr. became the first person executed by lethal injection in the United States, in Texas, on December 7, 1982 (Wikipedia, 2011a). Today, it is the most common form of execution in the United States.

The condemned person is usually bound to a gurney. Heart monitors are positioned on the inmate's skin to later help determine that death has occurred. Two needles are then inserted into usable veins, usually in the arms. (One needle is a backup.) Intravenous tubes connect the needles to several IV drips. The tubes are first flushed with saline, which is harmless. When the warden gives the signal, the executioners inject lethal doses of drugs into the IV tubes. Typically, the executioners are standing behind a curtain or are in another room and cannot be seen by the inmate or witnesses (Wikipedia, 2011h).

The first drug is an anesthetic, sodium thiopental, which puts the condemned into a deep sleep within thirty seconds. The recommended dose far exceeds the amount given to patients during operations. Some experts say this first dose is lethal and that the inmate feels nothing after that. Saline flushes the intravenous line once again before the next drug, pancuronium bromide, or Pavulon, is injected. This powerful muscle relaxer paralyzes the diaphragm and lungs. Over a period of one to three minutes, breathing stops.

In some but not all states that use lethal injection, a third saline flush occurs before the final drug is administered: a lethal dose of potassium chloride. This interrupts the electrical signaling essential to heart functions, which, in turn, induces cardiac arrest. Shortly afterward, a physician or medical technician pronounces the death. The amount of time between leaving the final holding cell and being pronounced dead may only be thirty minutes (Wikipedia, 2011h).

Brooks's execution by lethal injection was the first execution in Texas since 1964. The state that today executes more people than any other at one time took an almost twenty-year moratorium on capital punishment.

Brooks and an accomplice abducted a mechanic from a used-car lot and took him to a motel where he was bound and gagged and shot once in the head. The accomplice got forty years in prison. Brooks got the death penalty. While on death row, Brooks converted to Islam and, as his final statement, offered a prayer to Allah. The time between the date of his crime and his execution was one week short of six years (Wikipedia, 2011a).

6

Dead Inside

The rust-red-brick and gray Southern Indiana limestone façade of Mt. Vernon Township High School suggests that it was in many ways no different from other American high schools in 1985. The school was committed to serving the career needs of both vocational and academic students, striving for a balance between shop and technical classes and accelerated math and science offerings.

The school then as now carved out its regional identity as the Rams, according to which seasonal sport was being played. Students aligned themselves with the cliques that would help them establish and underscore their identities: the jocks, the brainiacs, and the stoners. Senior year in high school gave Tom Odle the opportunity to find himself and lose himself at the same time.

> When I was seventeen, the physical abuse pretty much stopped after I pushed my mother up against the hallway wall and told her there would be no more hitting me without me hitting back. She got a little scared and ran to my father, but he never said anything to me about it. But they were having their own problems as far as their marriage was going. My father worked from 4:00 P.M. to midnight, and while he was at work, my mother would be hanging out with her friends at bars or at the bowling alley. I didn't complain because if she was gone, I wouldn't have to deal with her. And of course, if she was gone, then I could leave my siblings at home by themselves.

Yvonne Sexton, Carolyn's best friend, testified for the prosecution during the sentencing phase of Tom's trial. Sexton was familiar with the activities of the children and some of the conflicts within the family. She testified that Tom had been accused of stealing a coin collection of his father's and about fifteen silver dollars that belonged to his mother. She reported that he kicked a hole in the kitchen wall during an angry telephone conversation, and he chased his brother Sean around the house with a knife. But no one was ultimately hurt. Sexton testified that she had seen bruises on Carolyn's back as a result of being pushed against a wall by Tom during an argument (*People of the State of Illinois vs. Thomas Odle*, 1986).

She also reported an incident at the Logan Street Church in which Tom was accused of ordering Sean and Scott to steal purses from cars in the church parking lot. When asked about the relationship between Tom and his mother, Sexton stated that Carolyn was frightened of Tom. She added that the other children were also afraid of him because he had hit them in the past. During cross-examination by the defense, Sexton agreed that Carolyn had had significant difficulty dealing with her children, in general, and she frequently placed responsibility for the care and safety of her three younger children in Tom's hands, requiring that he babysit the other children on an almost daily basis while she pursued her social obligations and recreational activities, such as bowling.

During redirect by the prosecution, Sexton testified that she was aware that Sean had been involved in antisocial activities as well, but she was unaware of such activities with regard to Robyn or Scott.

Years later, Sexton recalled an event involving Sean and Scott that, in part, precipitated the establishment of the final deadline by which Tom would have to leave the Odle home: "I worked with the church, Logan Street Baptist Church, at the time. It was only about a half block from my house, and on Wednesday nights, I would be there most of the evening because after school we had choir practice, and I played the piano for the choir. My kids and I would usually go up there and eat, and later on, we had a prayer service. Then I had my choir practice. Well, in between the choir practice, I ran home for something. When I came back to the church, I saw Sean and Scottie running, hiding behind a church bus. I told them, 'Come out from there, I saw you. What are you doing back there?' Well, they came out, and they were scared out of their minds. They said, 'We're going to get in trouble.' I said, 'Why, what are you doing? Who are you going to get in trouble with?' They said, 'Tommy.' And I said, 'Why?' And they said, 'Because we don't have any money or any credit cards to take home with us.' And I said, 'What do you mean?' They said, 'We get into unlocked cars and go through purses left in the cars.' And they didn't have anything to take home. They were afraid to go home. I said, 'You're coming home with me.' And I took them to my house" (personal communication, September 30, 2006).

After taking the boys to her house, Sexton called the Odle house "to try to get ahold of Carolyn. They had more than one phone, so Robyn, I think, answered the phone. But while I was talking to her, Tommy got on, too. I was trying to find Carolyn. They said that she had gone grocery shopping. Tommy said, 'I can take a message.' And, I said, 'No, I'll just call her later,' because I didn't want to say anything. So, I hung up the phone, and then I called Bob at work and told him what was going on with the kids. He said he was going to be talking to him [Tom]" (personal communication, September 30, 2006).

Light in the Darkness

At one point, each of my parents would tell me about the other. My mother would complain about my father to me, and my father would complain about my mother to me. That is, until one night I came home pretty drunk, and they said I cussed both of them out. Then I got into a slapping bout with my mother until my father had to break it up. Then, he and I got into it. I don't recall this, but I was told about it the next morning and was a bit sore from some kind of fight.

I never could understand the anger my mother had for me or the anger I had for my mother, because I would see other parents act differently towards their children, and I always longed for that type of interaction with my mother. Whenever I hugged my mother for any reason, she never hugged me back. She always became rigid and would not hug me back. I could never get past that in my head. That, and her always telling me what a disappointment I was and how she wished I had never been born and that she hoped I would die during the night so she wouldn't have to put up with me any longer. Even my father would talk about running away on his motorcycle, dumping it in a lake along with all of his iden- tification, and starting a new life. I never understood these things coming from my parents who were supposed to love me, for just me. But I never got it, or if I did, I never felt it.

Children and Family Services came and took my brother Sean and placed him in foster care because they caught my mother in the act of chaining my brother to the bed, as she had done for years. There had been counselors to the house working with my parents—mostly my mother—but she was very angry and unhelpful and did not go along with the program. I knew they came to the house and [I] would stay away so I wouldn't have to talk to them and feel like I was on trial. I knew if I said something against my mother, once they left, it would be hell on earth in that house. I think I got caught there maybe once when they came. Otherwise, I ran and hid until they were gone.

I think that's what kicked the separation between my parents. That coupled with her running out to bars while he was working. I recall one time I followed her to a lounge where she and her friend Yvonne were at. My mother was dancing with this guy who used to be friends with my parents. Something had happened along the way, and they were friends no longer. Anyway, she was dancing with him in a seductive way, so I called my dad and told him. He came out there and saw for himself what was going on. He went in there and almost got into a fight with this guy, but my mom stopped it and told him she would not be home if he hit this guy. My dad told her to go home, but she got smart with him. So my dad left and went back to work.

It was different after that. But I always liked the fact she finally got some of what she had been handing out to me all those years. She was put on the spot in front of her friends and got caught doing something she knew better than to do. They eventually split up after that incident, a few months later.

I was a senior in high school at that time. I was trying to plan for a future, but between breaking into houses and doing drugs, I never really got my mind on it. I was just going from day to day and not really planning on anything past that. I was enrolled in a building trades class where the class goes out and actually builds a house. I was really interested in it, but I was also getting high at the house and goofing off.

I was also skipping school more and stealing cars for joy rides. My parents would not let me drive yet by myself because I was still being punished for getting caught breaking into homes the first time. So, I walked everywhere or rode my bike. If I was on one side of town and wanted to get to the other side and didn't feel like walking, especially in the cold, I would try to find a car with keys in it. Or if I had some keys from one of the car dealer lots where I had stolen earlier, I would take one of those cars to get me to the other side of town and then leave it. I just didn't care about what happened to me. It was just what I could get at the moment to keep me satisfied for a little while. I was always looking to get high or any chance to do something crazy.

At about that time, I started openly smoking cigarettes at home. I was listening to metal music at the time, likely Motley Crue, Judas Priest, Ozzy, Black Sabbath, and Led Zeppelin. I had long hair, and I was going to concerts like Iron Maiden, Twisted Sister, and AC/DC. I also liked the classics, like the Rolling Stones, The Who, Eric Clapton, Cream, and other groups from the 70s and the 60s. I liked the blues and basically the guitar-driven music, be it hard driving riffs or slow riffs, just the guitar in general. The lyrics were not what attracted me to the music I listened to. It was the music, because some of the lyrics were pretty far out there for me, like not making sense or something, altogether way out of reality.

During this time I was drinking a little bit more. And, I was still smoking reefer, doing cocaine, and other drugs like heroin and LSD, on a regular basis. I was also doing PCP whenever I could get my hands on it. My mother took Valium, so I was also taking it whenever I could get away with it. I did not like my life. I did not like the people in my life. So I escaped every chance I could. I thought I had some good friends during that time, but they were just people that I got high with. Every time we got together it was to get high or find a way to get high.

As I mentioned before, I was seeing a girl at that time. There was no real connection there for me, but I knew she was really into me by the way she would hang all over me. It was cool but to be honest, I didn't like somebody hanging all over me all the time. So, we never really connected. Then I was off to the next girl.

But I have to admit, when I was with a girl, my criminal activities slowed down because of the time I would spend with the girl. It wasn't because I wanted to do good or anything like that. It was because I didn't have the time. My dad never questioned me about that night the girl got caught outside my window, and things just went on as usual. I was back into the criminal life of breaking in and getting high. I really liked cocaine and reefer together, and that is where a lot of my money went because I didn't have much else. I also had a large record collection, as I would go to yard sales and pick up old albums that were in good shape.

I was finally able to start driving by myself during the springtime of my senior year. At that time I was really cool with a girl named Sandy. We dated for about a week but were just better off friends. And we were the best of friends. I think my involvement with her was my first real relationship, because we didn't get high every time we got together. I would go to her house just to hang out, or I would take her out to eat. If neither of us had dates for the weekend, we would go out together, but only as friends. We never had sex. It was a cool relationship. I really think that was when I first realized about love because I can really say that I loved her and I knew she felt the same way.

I would have my dad's car every Sunday afternoon until Sunday night. I had to put gas in it, but that was nothing. That made me feel a little older and better among my peers because they were all driving or they had their own cars, and I felt somehow included in my teen peer group. It was nice to see people I knew out driving when I wasn't with one of my parents. I started getting into a few more fights than I usually did, but they were nothing. I remember one fight I got into at the mall because I said something about another guy's girlfriend. I ended up fighting him at the mall by the bathroom. Some people called the police, but they just took our names down and that was it, besides being banned from the mall.

I got into another fight at the park because this guy slapped Sandy. I chased him all over town before I caught up with him at the park. That one was not a pretty sight. I was winning the one-on-one fight until his friends jumped in on me. Before the crowd could break it up, they got me pretty good. So, of course, I had to go find them one by one and even things up a bit. I remember coming home after getting beat up pretty bad. My mom stopped me at the back door when she saw all the blood and told me I must have finally gotten what I deserved. I just laughed and went in and cleaned myself up. I went through the rest of my senior year just goofing off, really. [My friend] Ray lived across from the high school at the time. So I would end up there a lot of the time after skipping school.

I felt dead inside most of the time, back then. It was like there was nothing inside me, because everything I cared about doing was destroyed by my mother. And, anyone who ever showed an interest in me was run off by my mother. So, there was nothing and no one I truly connected with. I think the only reason Sandy and I got along so well was that she never came in direct contact with my mother. I had to keep her away from my mother. When she came to my house, my parents would be gone, and the rest of the time I would go to her house. I got along well with her parents, and I got along well with Ray's parents.

I did not graduate high school. I was one credit shy of graduating: a half credit for American history and another half credit for English. I was never good in English, and history bored me because I believed they were teaching me lies. So I was never interested. I started to go to summer school to make up the credits to get my diploma, but I ended up getting a job at Walt's Pizza. So, I quit school in the summer and started working part-time at Walt's Pizza.

I started dating a very special girl [name withheld] at that time. I had always liked her, but she was always with this one guy, so I never pushed it. One day we finally got together and it was good. It felt good to be with her and have her with me. She made me want to do good and be someone good. I had stopped seeing Linda. I wasn't doing so many drugs, and I had stopped breaking into houses. I wanted everything to be right. I was working a real job and spending every available moment I could with her. I was around my parents very little. I was eventually laid off at Walt's Pizza because it closed down. So, my dad got me a job with a lumber company loading trucks for delivery, working with customers, and picking up around the yard. I was able to get my own car and really felt good. I was doing less drugs and very little drinking. I was only smoking reefer and that was basically on the weekends, with very little through the week. I wasn't do-ing cocaine or anything else. I didn't even mind her coming around my parents, because I had told her they were nuts. I even got along well with her parents, and she got along well with mine, unbelievably. Her parents even took me on vaca-tion with them when they went to Kentucky Lake for a week. It was good and she and I were going smoothly.

Today, that "special girl" is an attractive, charming woman with san-dy-blonde hair and a warm smile. The time she spent with Tom Odle would leave an indelible mark on her life. They were introduced by a friend. "We both went to the same high school. I was fourteen. I knew who Tom was. We weren't acquainted. My friend said, 'Don't you know how to cut hair?' And I said, 'No, not really,' and he said, 'Well you're gonna have to try. Tom is trying to get a job at Walt's Pizza.' So I gave him a haircut, and he got a job and that's how we met. I believe we started dating not too long after, maybe within three months" (personal communication, September 30, 2006).

Her strongest memory of Carolyn Odle was of a time when she was in the Odle house, and Carolyn was not. "There was a basket of fruit on the kitchen table. I picked up an orange, and Tom turned white. He said, 'Oh my God, don't eat that!' I just looked at him like, 'Is it wax? Why?' He said, 'My mom will kill me. We are not allowed to eat anything without her permission.' He was scared. It was strange. I put it down. I'll never forget having that impression of her. Why can't her kids eat when she's not there? Why can't he eat an orange from this basket? I'll never forget that. He was scared" (personal communication, September 30, 2006).

> I got laid off at the lumber company because I was told I was too young for the union. I later found out that that was a lie. They thought I was lazy even though I thought I was doing a good job for them. I did what I was told and I guess that was the problem. They always had to tell me what to do because I wasn't used to working. I really didn't know what to do unless I was told what to do. So, I lost that job and felt really bad and stupid.
>
> She ["special girl"] got me a job working for her father. His company machined and welded wheels that were worn

down. I thought this was a good idea and went to work for her father. When I went to work for her father, I thought I was going to be doing something special. But instead, I was given the title of janitor, which did not sit right with me. I was supposed to pick up around the shop, clean the wheels before they were welded, and stuff like that, all for five dollars an hour. I didn't look at it as a place to start out and work my way up through the system, as I do now. It was an opportunity to make her father see me in a very good light. I saw it as being a janitor, which I did not like at all.

I worked there for about two and half months before I was fired for lying about cleaning some windows. I was told to clean some windows, and the next day they asked me if I had cleaned the windows. I lied and told them I had. So, I was fired. At that time, I didn't even care about the job because to me, it was a janitor job and I was above that.

Her father didn't like me anymore after that, which made things difficult on both of us when it came to getting together. That put some stress on her, as she had to hear what a no-good bum I was from her father all the time, and she didn't want to hear it. I also got caught going to a gas station and charging a tank of gas to her father's company. So, I messed things up pretty good and felt like shit because of it. But I didn't know how to get back in favor with her father.

Part of me just gave up, and I didn't even look for work. I wasn't hanging out with my friends, anymore. I was just hanging out with her. She and I never fought about anything. I got mad a couple of times because she wasn't where she usually was when I went to see her at school. She was a couple of years younger than me, and I would go to the school during the lunch hour to see her. Another time I got mad because one of her friends liked me and was trying to break us up. Her friend told me a bunch of stuff she was supposedly saying about me behind my back, which was not really anything. It did make me mad, but it didn't last long, and we survived it. We got along really good. I loved her, and I felt loved by her. She had to sneak around to see me because her father did not want her dating me at all anymore. But we kept seeing each other anyway.

Downward Spiral of Depression, Desperation, and Dejection

As a result of their growing frustration with their son, due to his lack of responsibility, repeated job failures, and general apathy, Carolyn and Bob Odle asked his girlfriend to assist them in their attempts to get Tom on the right track. "His parents came to me and said, 'Can you please help us? We love you and think you are wonderful for him. Can you help us get him to understand? We just want him to be more responsible, to understand how important it is to have a job and show up every day . . . to pay his car insurance and his gasoline and to straighten up.' Tom was upset with them, but they pulled me to the side and said, 'We don't know what to do'" (personal communication, September 30, 2006).

Years later, she reflected on her time with Tom and the Odle family. "Tom was not old enough to be on his own at that time. Children are just products of you. You raise your child, and they act this way or that way because that's how you raised your child. Some of it is inherited. Some of it is genetic. Some of it has to do with anxiety or depression. But most of the time when you point a finger at somebody, you are pointing three fingers back at yourself. Although I didn't witness abuse, I believe that it occurred. Children that act the way they did, it's obvious there was abuse. I would come over and the kids would just attack me. They loved me to death. Robyn would say that she wanted to grow up and be pretty, just like me. I always talked to the kids. I didn't just walk in the house and ignore them. I'd sit down and we'd go outside. As a matter of fact, on the day of the murders, I called his house to talk to his mother to see what the children wanted for Christmas that year. I was going to do some early shopping, but nobody answered the phone" (personal communication, September 30, 2006).

> About December, we found out she was pregnant, and it kind of ticked me off that she told her parents before she told me. Then I had to tell my father, who was supposed to call her dad and talk about a solution. She and I talked about running off and getting married someplace, but we had no money or anything and ended up having to go with the solution our fathers worked out. I either had to go in the army or face statutory rape charges because she was under age and I was seventeen at the time. It was enough to scare me into going in the army. Plus, my father thought it would be good for me. He thought I could learn a trade and get something good out of it.

My mother went crazy when she found out my girlfriend was pregnant and called me every name in the book.
She was happy that one part of the solution was for her to
get an abortion. Neither [my girlfriend] nor I wanted that,
but we had no choice and it happened. After that, her father
forbid me to ever see her again. So I started sneaking over to
her house at night when her parents were gone. We did that
for about three months until I had to leave for the army.

She and I were still together, but it was strained. I could
feel the strain her father was putting her through for sneaking out to be with me and lying in order to be with me. Her
parents knew she was lying to them about being with me as
we were seen together on several occasions.

In the meantime I was kicked out of my parents' house
just after Christmas because the tension between my mother
and me was really growing. After what my mom said about
the abortion, things got really tense. I was not very happy
with her and she knew it. She wanted me out of the house.
My father went along with it, and I went to stay with my
grandmother. Shortly after that, my father filed for divorce
from my mother, and he came to stay with his mother,
also. At that time, my father and I got to know one another,
finally, without the influence of my mother. We worked out
a lot of stuff, and we talked a lot about different things, like
what I had been through with her and everything else.

I thought I was doing the right thing about going into
the army because my girlfriend said she would wait for
me and be faithful. And her dad would have let her see me
again when I came home on leave. My dad was happy I was
learning some sort of job trade and some self-discipline. First
time I ever flew on a plane was going to Fort Dix, New Jersey,
where I did my basic training. I was cool there, actually. I
wasn't missing anybody except my girlfriend.

I was able to talk to her about twice a week. Then
things just started sounding strange between us. She started
telling me how much she missed me and that she wanted
me to come home. So I started asking questions about how
to get discharged and went through the motions, and out of
the army I came. But while I was there, I was cool. I mean I
didn't want to come out because I didn't like it or couldn't

hack it. I did it because my girlfriend was missing me. I was in good shape. I was working out and I had stopped smoking. I was lifting weights, also. I missed expert on the shooting range by one target. I was involved and doing what I thought was great. I had signed up to become a diesel mechanic after basic training.

My knees were always bad to begin with, but not so bad as to keep me out of the army. So I used them to get out. I was released with a medical honorable discharge, given some money and a ticket home, all after about two months of being there. I've thought a lot about the things I could have done if I had had the mindset I have now. To this day, I wish I would have stayed there and continued on. I would be getting out right about now and collecting a pension, while moving on to another job for the next twenty years. Then I could retire and collect two pensions.

I came home and my parents picked me up at the airport in St. Louis and drove me home. The next day I found out that my parents had gotten remarried while I was in the army. I wasn't happy or angry. I had no feelings about it either way. Of course, I called my girlfriend to tell her I was home, and she was on her way over to see me. My dad and I walked over to my grandmother's house so I could say hello and show off my uniform.

My girlfriend came and gave me a huge hug and kiss that told me I did the right thing by coming home, as she needed me. Then, she said we needed to talk. So we went to talk, which ended up with her breaking up with me. I didn't know what to think about this. I just sat there like a stupid idiot not saying a word. I was shocked. I felt my heart break at that point: It broke and shattered right then. I told her she needed to leave. I found out later that she was with a guy who had been coming over while I was gone. I think she dated him for a while after we broke up.

I got my car keys and with a few hundred dollars from the army, I was out to party. I went and got my old party friends and off to party land I went. I got something to drink. I got something to smoke. And I got anything else I could get my hands on. I just went around seeing people I knew and getting high. I bought some new clothes and just relaxed

because it was summer time and I was not going to stay
broken up about all that happened. But once everything wore
off, I was broken. It was like the wind had been taken out of
my sails. While I was in the army, my mom had my dog put
to sleep because she didn't want to take care of it. Everything
was just really screwed up for me from there on out. I was
really dead inside.

I went back to doing whatever drug was available. I was
like that from the time I woke up until I went to sleep, or I
passed out. I didn't care which came first. I was told I had
overdosed a few times because I didn't know when to stop
and didn't care if I ever did stop. For money, my friends and
I were breaking into local factories and homes, especially the
homes of people who sold drugs, because I was after their
drugs. I was after the drugs they were selling. I sold enough to
keep some pocket change, but I was doing everything I took.

It became well known that I always had drugs. I was
getting shot at sometimes, and they even tried to rob me
a few times. But I always had luck in getting away. I even
started carrying around this .25 automatic. I stole it out of a
car one night. I had a guy pull a gun on me, right in my face,
and pulled the trigger. But it hit the tree next to me instead.
I don't know how in the hell he missed me because that
barrel was pointed right at me. I wasn't scared though. That
is the thing I do not get. I was not scared at all. I was almost
hoping I would die to end the life that my mother had always
told me was worthless, anyway.

Maybe my parents sensed I was going nowhere, and I
was kicked out of the house again and I went to stay with
my grandmother. I needed some quick cash and ended up
taking some money out of her purse. After that my grandmother didn't trust me. Plus, I was always coming in high or
drunk because I didn't care one way or another. My grandmother could not take it, I guess, and my parents came to
take me back home and hopefully get straightened out. But
I didn't straighten out. I even wrote a suicide note to my
former girlfriend that I never mailed, because I shot a hole in
the ceiling while I was playing Russian roulette. My dad took
the gun away, and we never spoke about it. But I was asked
to leave, again.

MASS MURDER HERE, front-page headline, *Register-News* (Mt. Vernon, Illinois), November 9, 1985, one day after the Odle family murders.

Odle family photo, summer of 1985. *Top row, left to right*: Scott, 10; Sean, 13; Robyn, 14; *bottom row, left to right*: Tom, 18; Carolyn, 39; Robert, 39. Courtesy of the *Southern Illinoisan*, November 12, 1985; published with permission.

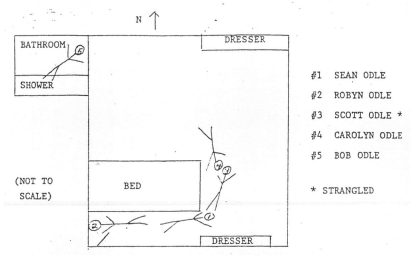

Police sketch of the crime scene.

People v. Odle, 1986.

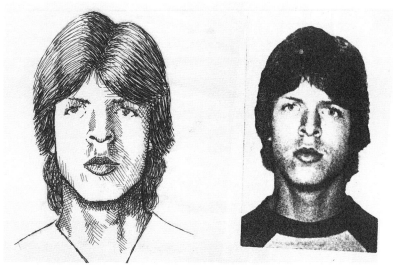

Sketch and arrest photo of Tom Odle, November 10, 1985.

Courtesy of the *Southern Illinoisan*, November 10, 1985; published with permission.

Tom Odle's depiction of his murdered family. Dr. Michael Althoff conducted the Draw-a-Family Test with Tom during a forensic psychological evaluation on April 9, 1986. *People v. Odle*, 1986.

Tom Odle, 19, being escorted to jail from the Richland County Courthouse on May 13, 1986, during his trial for the murders of his parents, two brothers, and sister. Courtesy of the *Southern Illinoisan*; published with permission.

Tom Odle, 19, after he was sentenced to death in July 1986 for the November 8, 1985, slayings. Courtesy of the *Southern Illinoisan*; published with permission.

Horace Mann Elementary School, Mt. Vernon, Illinois. All four Odle children attended Horace Mann, where Carolyn Odle was president of the PTO at the time of the Odle family murders. Courtesy of Mt. Vernon School District 80; published with permission.

Mt. Vernon Township High School, 1985. Tom Odle attended the high school but did not graduate. After murdering his parents on the morning of November 8, 1985, Tom drove to the high school to pick up his girlfriend. Courtesy of *Vernois*, 1985 yearbook, Mt. Vernon Township High School; published with permission.

Menard Correctional Center, Illinois Department of Corrections, Chester, Illinois. Tom Odle was confined to the condemned unit at Menard from 1986 to 1997. A maximum-security prison opened in 1878 as Southern Illinois Penitentiary, Menard Correctional Center was one of three Illinois prisons that housed death-row inmates. Infamous inmates included serial murderer John Wayne Gacy and mass murderer James Degorski. Wikipedia, 2011i; "Menard Correctional Center." Courtesy of the Illinois Department of Corrections; published with permission.

Cell house, Menard Correctional Center. Courtesy of the Illinois Department of Corrections; published with permission.

Falling Apart, Tom Odle, death-row art.
Published with permission.

Pontiac Correctional Center, Illinois Department of Corrections, Pontiac, Illinois. Tom Odle was confined to Pontiac's condemned unit from 1997 to 2002. A maximum-security prison opened in 1871, formerly known as the State Reformatory, Pontiac was one of three Illinois prisons that housed death-row inmates. Wikipedia, 2011k. Courtesy of the Illinois Department of Corrections; published with permission.

Cell block, Pontiac Correctional Center. Courtesy of the Illinois Department of Corrections; published with permission.

Tom Odle, 2003. Illinois Department of Corrections inmate photo taken after commutation of his death sentence to natural life. Published with permission.

F-House, Stateville Correctional Center, Illinois Department of Corrections, Joliet, Illinois. Tom Odle was confined to Stateville from 2003 to 2005. The maximum-security prison opened in 1925 and included some cell houses, such as F-House, commonly referred to as the Roundhouse, whose design was based on the panopticon architectural concept popularized in England during the eighteenth century. All executions by lethal injection in Illinois prior to 1998 were conducted at Stateville. Infamous inmates included Nathan Leopold, Richard Loeb, and Richard Speck. Wikipedia, 2011m. Courtesy of the Illinois Department of Corrections; published with permission.

Tom Odle, 2008. Illinois Department of Corrections inmate photo. Published with permission.

Girl in Café, Tom Odle, oil painting, 2007. Published with permission.

Winter Landscape, Tom Odle, oil painting, 2008. Published with permission.

Woman Dressing, Tom Odle, oil painting, 2009.
Published with permission.

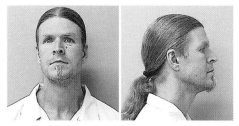

Tom Odle, 2011. Illinois Department of Corrections inmate photos; published with permission.

Odle family graves, Memorial Gardens Cemetery, Mt. Vernon, Illinois.
Photo by author.

So, I went to Kentucky where I knew this guy from the army who faked his way out of the army, also. His name was Clay, and I stayed with him for a while until I could get on my feet. I got a job working for this renovation company. I was making about five dollars an hour, plus all the overtime I wanted. I had stopped doing drugs for the most part only because I didn't know anyone there like I did at home. I was drinking like a fish, though. I was drinking every night and had hooked up with this really cute girl who liked hard drugs, just like me. I never missed work, and at night I was on the town. I was even going to strip clubs, and the girl was always with me. I think her name was Lisa. I was just getting up going to work, doing my little drug scene or drinking, and having sex with Lisa.

I was there for a couple of months or so. Then, his parents asked me to leave. I think Clay was stealing money from his mother and then blamed me for it. But I couldn't say anything about it. So I took the ticket back home and of course told Lisa goodbye, after trying to convince her to come back with me. But she couldn't leave. So, I gave Clay a very dirty look as he dropped me off at the bus station because he knew then that I knew what was going on. I had seen him taking some money, but I never thought anything of it, until I was asked to leave. I was really pissed at how they did me there in Kentucky. For once, I was doing something I enjoyed and was good at. It wasn't like anyone could say I was lazy or didn't know what to do, or had to be trained, as I knew everything about renovation.

I had no intention of going back home, but I was left with no choice, once again. I stayed with my grandmother again for a little while. I really had the same attitude as before, and I was with the same people before I left, getting high.

This time I even took a couple of my grandmother's checks from her checkbook and wrote them out to myself, totaling about $175. I really hadn't planned on being around too much longer as suicide was becoming the avenue I was going to take. I was just tired of everything going on around me. But needless to say, I was not able to go through with the suicide and was caught for the checks I wrote. My grandmother didn't press charges, but she made me go get my

GED, which I did without any problems. I never studied for the test or anything. I just walked in off the street and took the test. I passed it and got my GED. I really didn't feel any different after that. But I guess my parents were proud that I was at least able to get a GED.

After that I was invited back home with a huge speech that we should stick together. So, I moved back home. But after one week of me really trying to get along with everyone, I was once again asked to leave. And I was told that I could not go to either of my grandparents' homes or other relatives. If I did, they would call the police and have me arrested. That time, I believed them. So, that night I slept in the park. But I got tired of that and found an empty house, broke into it, and spent the night in the house.

The next day I went home to speak with my dad about the whole thing. I ended up being able to stay there another few days, until I could get a plan together of where I should go and so forth. However, I did no planning about where to go, how to get there, or what I was going to do afterwards. I just sat around and got high. I felt I was at my wits end and that I should go ahead with the suicide, but I just couldn't push myself to do it. I just didn't know what to do about it. Then, they set a deadline for me to be gone by Friday, when my father went to work.

With a mixed sense of desperation and relief, Carolyn shared the news of Tom's imminent departure from the Odle home with her friend Yvonne Sexton, who related: "Carolyn told me that Tom was told he had one week to move out. He had caused enough disruption in their home and must leave. He had to be out by that Friday. And his dad, for the first time, really meant business. He took the upper hand" (personal communication, September 30, 2006).

Tom describes himself at seventeen and eighteen as feeling "dead inside most of the time," but the one bright spot during that period of his life was his relationship with his girlfriend at the time. Nevertheless, his increasing depression and drug abuse, combined with his repeated failures in attempts to live on his own, away from home, perpetuated the downward spiral of psychological disintegration that had begun two years earlier.

Tragically, at the age of eighteen, Tom was falling fast without a net in a downward spiral of dejection and desperation from which he would not recover. Ultimately, the intense sense of abandonment that he felt in reaction to his parents' demand that he move out of the house once and for all compelled the eighteen-year-old to commit an unthinkable and unforgivable crime.

Insanity and Executions

During Tom Odle's senior year in high school, the U.S. Supreme Court ruled that states could not execute the insane, as they are incapable of understanding the nature and consequences of the death penalty. The Court determined that this violated the Eighth Amendment's ban on "cruel and unusual punishment." The landmark case was *Ford v. Wainwright*, 477 U.S. 399 (1986).

Alvin Bernard Ford was tried and convicted of killing a police officer during a restaurant robbery in Fort Lauderdale, Florida, in 1974. In 1982, fourteen hours before he was to be executed, the U.S. Court of Appeals ordered a delay. His lawyer claimed that Ford had gone insane while on death row awaiting execution (Wikipedia, 2011c).

By that time, Ford had begun referring to himself as Pope John Paul III. He claimed, among other things, that he thwarted attempts by prison guards to torture his female relatives inside the prison, uncovered and foiled a Ku Klux Klan conspiracy to bury dead prisoners inside the prison walls, and appointed nine new Florida supreme-court justices. Ultimately, a panel of three psychiatrists examined him and concluded that while he did suffer from various mental disorders, including psychosis, he was still capable of understanding the nature of his crime and its punishment. Florida Governor Daniel Robert "Bob" Graham signed Ford's death warrant in 1984. But the appeals continued (Wikipedia, 2011c).

In 1989, a Florida judge determined that Ford was sane. His attorneys were appealing that ruling when Ford died of natural causes in 1991. But the legal precedent for lack of competence to be executed, based on insanity, remains on the books.

7

Murder: November 8, 1985

When Carolyn Odle left her house that morning to fulfill her community duties at the elementary school and run a few errands, she grabbed her jacket on her way out the door. It had been unseasonably warm for Southern Illinois. But it was still November, two weeks from Thanksgiving, and it was like Carolyn to be prepared should the weather turn cold.

As usual, Bob Odle worked the night shift and woke up after his wife and three of his children were gone. He put on a T-shirt and blue jeans and went to the kitchen to fix his breakfast.

> The day before the crime, I was feeling like I had nowhere
> to go and nobody to turn to for help. I had been told to stay
> away from all family members, as they wanted nothing to do
> with me. All my life growing up when something bad would
> happen to me like getting beaten or having to go without a
> meal, or having something taken away or destroyed, I would
> often think "I wish they were dead." But I had never sat down
> and planned it out or wanted to be the cause of their death.
> I just wanted it to happen. And this was no exception to
> the rule of wanting them all dead. I wanted to be rid of the
> connection, the pull, the hold that I always felt they had on
> me. They never let me grow in my own direction, because I
> was never really allowed to do very much growing up unless
> I was sneaky about it and lied about it afterwards. So, that
> became the standard style of interaction with my parents.

> But I never actually wanted them dead. And, I never actually
> wanted to be the cause of their death. It was just my anger
> boiling up and me thinking mad, that's all.

On the last day of her life, Carolyn presumed that her son Tom would be gone the next day. She didn't know where he was going to go because he didn't know where he was going to go. And he probably wouldn't tell her if he did. The family was through with him. He was no longer welcome at his grandmother's house.

Tom and his father had yet another argument the day before, and Bob had finally drawn the line. He had ordered Tom to be out of the house by 4:00 P.M. and said he would be taking the boy's clothes with him when he left for work on Friday. According to Carolyn's best friend, Yvonne Sexton, both Carolyn and Bob hoped that kicking Tom out of the house would force him to get his act together. Carolyn was glad that Bob was finally taking a stand with her against Tom. From Carolyn's perspective, Tom clearly knew how to pull his father's strings and elicit his support. Tom had done it time after time since he was a young child. But she wouldn't be at peace until Tom was gone for good (personal communication, September 30, 2006).

> That morning, I did my usual routine of getting up around
> mid-morning, smoking a joint, then a cigarette, then taking
> a shower, and smoking some more weed after I took my
> shower. It seemed that was the only way I could function in
> or out of the house. And, if it wasn't weed, then it was what-
> ever I could get my hands on to numb the real world and the
> problems in it. The night before, I had picked up a couple
> hits of acid, white blotter I think it was, for ten dollars. I was
> going to start the day with an acid trip because I had the feel-
> ing that it was going to be my last day, anyway. I didn't care
> about anything, and I wanted to be dead, anyway. I seemed
> to not be able to do anything right, anymore.

Every morning from 8:30 to 10:30 A.M., Carolyn volunteered as assistant to the school librarian. On the morning of the day she died, she was running late and was distressed about the situation with Tom.

The school librarian was aware that Carolyn was an avid bowler and actively involved in the local bowling league. Carolyn rarely discussed her personal affairs or disclosed her feelings about Tom or her other children. But it was well known that she loved bowling and she was apparently very good at it. Bowling was the fulcrum of her social life. She was an officer in the bowling league and typically bowled two or three evenings per week. To those who knew about her socially isolated and oppressive upbringing, bowling represented the conduit to a social life that she had always desired.

Given her fondness for bowling and her commitment to the school library, she was allowed to hold bowling-league meetings in the library. She had scheduled one such meeting that morning, and despite her concerns regarding Tom, she held the meeting because she took such responsibilities very seriously. After a brief meeting, she was off to run her morning errands and planned to return home before Bob left for work.

The PTO also held its meetings in the school library, and as president of the PTO, Carolyn was in even more frequent contact with the library staff. She had a creative, artistic flair and was asked to design the library bulletin boards. Initially, her designs were elaborate patterns with bright, colorful images and cheerful messages. However, as the tension between Carolyn and Tom mounted and the turmoil within the Odle household increased, the bulletin boards grew darker and gloomier. Despite encouragement from the library staff to produce big, flashy, colorful designs that would catch the eye and grab the attention of the students, her designs began to reflect her darkening mood, emotional distress, and preoccupation with her son Tom. And, as a result of the heightened stress she experienced during the last few days of her life, she informed the school personnel that she had developed hives.

The Murders

When I went into the kitchen that morning, my father was sitting at the table still eating his breakfast. So, I walked to the sink, and there was this voice in my head telling me to get the knife that was on the wall. The voice was not a strange voice. It was my voice and it had an angry tone. So, I got the knife and put it in my pants so my father wouldn't see it as I went back to my room. But I never went to my room. I stopped in the hall closet and sat there wondering why I had grabbed this knife. Because it was crazy to think I was going to do anything with it. It was like having an argument with myself about what to do with this knife. So, I ended up carving on my forearm while this argument was going on in my head.

Finally, I just got up to put the knife back in the rack and leave to go find some more weed or acid, or something. But on the way to where the knife was to be placed, my father got up and stood there in my way, preventing me from getting to the rack without him seeing me with the knife. So, I turned the corner and went into the living room and tried to put the knife behind the couch to hide it, thinking that I would put it up later when my father wasn't looking.

But my voice was yelling and screaming in my head to do it the whole time I was trying to hide the knife. It would not shut up. Then, the next thing I remember I'm standing there and there is blood everywhere, flowing out of my father's neck. I froze because I could not believe it was really happening. The voice in my head that had been screaming to do it was finally quiet, but I was frozen and scared because I didn't know if this was real or what.

I was frozen until my father walked to the phone and said that we needed to call for help. But I just took the phone away because I was scared and in shock. I couldn't think of what to do or say. I just remember looking at him and him looking at me, and he told me that he loved me. But that did not help, as my father had never told me that all my life. I was still trying to figure out if this was real or not. So, I walked up to him, but not very close and looked at all the blood everywhere. When I turned my back to him to look out the window for some reason, he slid out of the chair and onto the floor. I knew then he was gone. So, I grabbed his feet and drug him into the master bathroom. At that point, it clicked that I had to clean up the kitchen, because of the mess.

One can only imagine how Carolyn felt while driving home during the final minutes of her life. She probably wondered if Tom would ever amount to anything. He was lazy and disrespectful. She knew he took drugs. And he was a liar. She was so disappointed in her son. But she and Bob had given Tom all the chances that they were going to give him. Now she was done. They were throwing him out of the house to force him to make it on his own. She knew he had the ability to be self-sufficient. If he would just try, he'd be OK. She wasn't looking forward to these last few hours with Tom in the house. Thank God, Bob was there. She did not want to be alone with Tom.

My mom was supposed to be home at 11:30 and there was this blood all over the floor and I thought, "ah man, it's going to be wild." So, I hurried it up and tried to clean it up. Well, I got most of it—I got it cleaned up off the floor with a mop and then put some 409 on it.

There were no thoughts going through my mind when I was cleaning up the mess. It was just weird. It was as if I was being controlled by something, until my mother pulled up. Then my voice, that was yelling at me earlier to do it, was back telling me that we have to finish it all now that it has started. So, I just went along with it.

At approximately 10:30 A.M., Carolyn pulled into the driveway of her home at 1005 South Twenty-Third Street. She may have sat in the car thinking about the path her life had taken. She and Bob had weathered family storms before. They had split up but then remarried, and their relationship was stronger than ever. Today, they would have to be strong and stand united in order to get Tom out of the house. She would not allow Bob to buckle under pressure from Tom to let him stay. She stepped out of her car, walked to the back of the house, and reached for the door.

I hid behind the back door where she comes in and when she came in, just as she looked at me, I stabbed her in the neck. She ran to the living room and I attacked her all the way. Then she got away from me and threw her keys at me. She asked me if I was trying to kill her and I told her "yup." Then, she fell right there in front of the master bedroom door and I just dragged her in the bedroom. I said, "look at dad." And then she just fell down. I dragged her over and laid her at the foot of the bed.

I went through her purse for some cash, and I grabbed the car keys. But before I left, I saw all the blood all over the furniture, so I had to clean it up. I cleaned it up. Then I noticed I had blood all over me. So, I washed up real quick, changed my clothes, and put them in the washing machine.

According to Tom's confession the day after the murders, he was wearing jeans, a black AC/DC T-shirt, and Nike tennis shoes when he murdered his parents. He washed and dried the jeans because he thought he would wear them later. He put on camouflage pants and a blue T-shirt that read "Charging Charlie" before he left the house.

> And off I went to pick up my friend Larry and his girlfriend, Kim. I usually went to the high school by lunchtime to see the girl I was dating at the time, Theresa. I was in my father's car. I used to drive it before I had gotten my own car. But I had sold my car, and I had no insurance. And, I wasn't allowed to drive any of my parents' cars for that reason.
>
> So, I had my father's car and picked up my friends. Off to the high school we went to meet Theresa and just drive around the school, be seen, and all that stuff that young people do. I bought some weed there. I think it was a quarter ounce. Since Kim was pregnant, she didn't smoke weed. But Larry and I were smoking, and Theresa a little bit. She was never fond of my drug habits, but I suppose she tolerated them, since she stayed with me. After we cruised around for a while, I took Larry and Kim back to Kim's house, and then I took Theresa back to school. We made plans to spend the night in a motel. We had been talking about it for some time but just never really got it planned out.
>
> I was still not sure what was going on at home. It was like it was real, but it was like I was looking through someone else's eyes because it didn't seem like me or feel like me. It was as if I became someone else whenever I got home. I don't know how else to explain it. There was no formulation of a plan or even an idea as to how to do it or what to use, or what to do afterwards. It just happened. Everything was on the spur of the moment, and the decisions were made then and there as it was unfolding. There were no "if this happens, then that happens." I didn't think about punishment alternatives should I get caught. Those thoughts did not cross my mind. I just felt like I was living through someone else's eyes and something else was guiding me through the day because it did not seem real to me at all.
>
> I sound like a broken record to myself when I continually ask myself what caused me to do something like that. Because there was no formulation of a plan, no weighing of the punishment, and there was no decision to commit those acts in advance. This was my struggle with myself. If there

had been a plan, I would probably feel better knowing that
I had made a conscious decision, got caught, and am now
being punished for committing those crimes. But instead, I
recall the day like an old movie I saw on TV. It just doesn't
sound or feel like me. It took me a while to really accept that
this happened.

        I was worried that somebody was going to come by the
house because I didn't tell anybody because I didn't want
anybody to know. I got home about 2 o'clock. I watched a little bit of TV. Cleaned up a little bit . . . cleaned the blood off
of the TV, off the refrigerator, the floor, the table and chairs.

Sexton's brief encounter with Tom on the day of the murders would haunt
her for many years to come. Unaware that Carolyn and Bob already lay
dead inside, she arrived at the Odle home to share some news with her
friend. "The day he was supposed to be out was the day he killed them.
I came by the house that day because Carolyn came to the school that
morning, but she wasn't feeling well. I'm sure it was an emotional thing
for her, all that was going on, with her son being forced out of the house.
I'm sure she was having a hard time dealing with it. Normally, I wouldn't
have gone over to their house, but I hadn't heard from my parents for a
while. They had been on a trip to the Bahamas, and I was kind of upset
because I hadn't heard from my mom. Carolyn said, 'If you don't hear from
them soon, I'm going to call them myself and tell them they need to call
you, because you're upset.' You know, she was concerned about me. But
I had gotten a letter in the mail from my mom that day, and I was taking
it over to show her because I was excited. So, I went to their house, and
Tommy came out and met me at my car. I didn't even get all the way out
of my car. I had one foot on the gravel and one foot in my car. And he
was talking to me. And I said, 'Well, where is your mom?' Because her car
was there, both cars were still there. And he said, 'Oh, she went to lunch
with a friend.' And I said, 'Do you know when she'll be back?' And he
said, 'No, but I'm sure she'll call you.' It seemed perfectly fine. I knew she
had a friend coming into town, and maybe they were spending the whole
day together. So, I didn't think anything of it" (personal communication,
September 30, 2006).

      After I dropped Theresa off, I went back home to smoke
      some weed. I was feeling the acid pretty good by that time.
      I also found some Jack Daniels in the house and went to

drinking that. I think I drank about half a pint real quick, but I ended up throwing it back up after a while. I never was really a drinker and couldn't hold alcohol very well. So, I went back to smoking the weed that I had gotten while I was at the high school. I was smoking the joints as if they were cigarettes. Back then I was smoking maybe a pack and a half a day. I didn't smoke very many cigarettes that day.

I was sitting there rolling and smoking when my little brother came home from school. We lived only a few blocks from the grade school, so my little brother Scott walked home most every day unless it was really cold out. Just before Scott came home, Yvonne, my mother's friend, stopped by the house and wanted to show my mother some pictures. But I stepped out on the porch and told her that she wasn't home. She said she would catch up with her later on and she left. Then Scott came home about a half hour later.

When he got home, we just sat and talked about school, and he asked where Mom and Dad were. I told him they were gone for the moment. I had towels down on the floor where I had drug my dad in there on the floor. I told him it *[the blood]* was paint.

We were just sitting there talking and watching television, and then I told him to come back to our room for a second because there was something I wanted to show him. My intention was to show him something I had just gotten the night before. But on the way back there, something came over me, and the next thing I knew I had his neck in my hands, squeezing. I was squeezing so hard it caused cramps in my hands and forearms. So, I grabbed this pajama top or bottom and tied it around his neck and drug him into the master bedroom where my mother was. I stood there and looked at them. I didn't know what to do anymore, as this was out of control and I couldn't stop myself. I think it was then I decided to kill myself when it was all done.

It was like I knew my other brother and sister were going to meet the same fate. And, I had decided to do it also. I had to finish it all, with me being the last one to go. But I wanted one night to myself, as if I meant something. Larry called and shook me out of my daze and asked if I was coming to pick them up. I told him I'd pick them up at about 4:30 or so. Then we hung up, and I went to go pick up my sister and brother from school. I remember almost getting into a couple of accidents while driving to pick them up, but somehow I managed to avoid an accident. I was driving in the middle of the tracers I was seeing, hoping I would stay on the road.

While Tom drove his father's car to the school to pick up Robyn and Sean, Sexton returned to the Odle home: "I went to pick up my kids from school and went back over to the house because I figured the kids would be home by then. But Bob's car was gone, and Carolyn's car was still there. So, I thought she was home. I went around the house, because they had this house where the bedrooms were in the back and that's where everyone went when they got home. I knew if I knocked on the front door they might not hear me. But I couldn't get any response from anyone. So I left and I didn't go back. I believe that during that time he was picking up Robyn and Sean with his dad's car" (personal communication, September 30, 2006).

Once we got home I knew what was going to happen. I couldn't even look at my brother Sean, nor did I want him to see me. So, I blindfolded him and I think I tied his hands behind his back. I don't know why I tied his hands, but I do know I didn't want him to look at me or see what I was doing. I remember stabbing him a couple of times, although during the trial they said it was numerous times. Again, that same angry voice was telling me how it just had to be done.

I had walked out of the room to collect myself and try to shake everything off when I heard stumbling around. When I opened the door, Sean was up and walking around with blood all over his face, with the blindfold off and his hands undone. He was holding his throat and waving his hands. I freaked out and I just started stabbing him in the head a lot and the back of the neck. He fell down right next to Scott and didn't move anymore after that.

I kept asking myself what was going on, but there was no answer. Inside myself I did not want this to happen, but it would not stop. I could not stop myself. Once I walked out of the bedroom, I went and got my sister. I put my hand over her eyes and walked her to the bedroom. I told her I had a surprise for her. She goes, "This better be a good surprise." I took my hand off her eyes and said, "surprise."

She turned pale; she turned very, very pale. I thought
she was going to have a heart attack right there and then.
Then she started hollering at me. "Don't do it. Don't do it.
Let me go." I told her I couldn't because she had already seen
them. So I stabbed her in the neck four or five times, and
stabbed her in the side. She fell on the bed and there was
blood just gushing out of her neck. It was going all over the
bed. And then she just plopped in the corner.

I felt ashamed but it wasn't enough to stop me from
doing to her what I had done to everyone else in my family,
the family I belonged to. The angry me-voice stopped yelling
at me once I walked out of the bedroom.

I had blood all over me, all over my face, my hands: cut
my hands real bad when I was stabbing him [Sean] in the
head. I took a shower, changed my clothes, grabbed some
money off the dresser, and off I went. I locked up everything
and was going to live my last night with some friends and
my girlfriend.

Tom placed the butcher knife on the dresser in the bedroom within a
few feet of the bodies of his family. He took about $15 from his mother's
purse and another $7 from his father's pants pocket. Then he locked the
backdoor and left the house. It was 4:15 P.M. He had almost made the 4:00
deadline to be out of the house.

After he closed the back door, silence filled the Odle house. His home,
the scene of many arguments, accusations, and altercations, was still.

Tom walked around the house and once again got in his father's car,
a 1978 Mercury Marquis. He had not been allowed to drive his father's
car since he had returned from the army. It was off limits. But now, finally, there were no limits. He drove around town for a while and picked
up Larry and Kim. Then he drove to the gas station across from the
Burger King to pick up Theresa. She got in, and they continued to cruise
around town for another hour. Earlier, they had made plans to spend the
night at the Travel Inn Motel, a Tenth Street motel. They arrived there at
about 6:30 P.M.

I picked up Larry and Kim. We smoked some weed on
the way to pick up Theresa at a gas station, where she was
waiting for me. We went to Larry's brother's place where I
started really getting higher. Then, I went out and bought

some more weed for the night, as well as some dust. I think I bought another quarter ounce of weed. We left there after smoking some weed, and I went and found a motel room for Theresa and me for the night. I got the room and remember the clerk having to count out the money because I couldn't do it myself, since I was so high. I don't know if I was still tripping or not.

We went to the room; Theresa, Larry, Kim and myself were all there. Theresa had had enough weed, so Larry and I started smoking by ourselves while the girls watched movies on the T.V. After a while, Kim was ready to go home. So, I took Kim and Larry home while Theresa stayed at the motel room. I don't think either one of us went to sleep for very long, if at all. I just couldn't sleep at all. I just laid there while I tossed and turned all night. I kept thinking if what had happened that day was real or not because it did not seem real at all. I could not get over the feeling that something bad had happened and I was responsible, but I couldn't accept that what had happened really happened. I was thinking I was on a bad trip and that what I thought had happened was just some imaginary movie playing in my head. But when we got up the next morning, Theresa called her friend who told her that the police were looking for both of us. At that instant, I knew it was real and that I was going to have to kill myself, in order to complete the circle.

Crime Scene and the Coroner's Findings

According to Jefferson county coroner Dr. Richard Garretson, Bob Odle lay in the master bathroom, separate from his wife and three children, who were in the master bedroom. Garretson describes the scene: "You could actually see drag patterns of blood going around the bed and toward the bathroom and then there was a large pool of blood under the father's neck and head in the bathroom.

"The fatal wound . . . was above the right collar bone and transected . . . across the jugular vein. The carotid artery itself had not been lacerated or cut, but the jugular vein itself, which is a vein as big as my thumb perhaps three quarters of an inch in diameter, had been cut across. This is where the mass majority of blood loss occurred. At the time of the autopsy . . . we observed within the heart cavity a large amount of air, which tends to occur when the jugular vein is cut across. It tends to create a sucking wound so that as the person breathes in and out, as they inhale and decrease the interthoracic pressure, the air is sucked in from the jugular vein into the heart." This type of wound, Dr. Garretson observed, was present in other family members as well. All of the stabbing victims had defensive wounds as well (*People of the State of Illinois vs. Thomas Odle*, 1986).

Bob was lying on his back with his feet on the edge of the bathtub. The sad expression that he carried in death reflected the final realization that his troubled eldest son would actually take his father's life. Bob's white T-shirt was almost completely red; his skin was extremely pale, both due to massive blood loss. Remarkably, he was still wearing his glasses. His eyes were open.

Carolyn lay dead at the foot of her bed. Dr. Garretson said in testimony: "She had three lacerations on the right lower side of her neck going at a stepladder fashion from the area of the collar bone to the upper portion, her mid-portion of the neck and into the upper portion of the neck on the right side.

"The upper portion of her garment was saturated with blood and there was some blood pooling under her right shoulder. The wounds were basically covered by heavy layers of blood, and one could perceive a wound there but you couldn't see it accurately because of the amount of blood that covered both the neck and the upper portion of the shirt.

"The lower wound on the right side of her neck cut the junction of the internal jugular vein with the right subclavian vein coming from the right arm. The middle wound lacerated the internal jugular vein [and] again the large jugular vein and the upper wound transected the carotid artery on the right side. . . . Any one of these wounds would have caused death" (*People of the State of Illinois vs. Thomas Odle*, 1986).

Her pale and lifeless face no longer reflected the expression of shock that she must have experienced as her son attacked her or the horror she must have felt when she saw her dead husband just before she died. Her eyes remained open but now held only the blank stare of the dead. Her right hand rested against the head of her youngest son, Scott.

Scott still had the yellow pajama bottoms used to end his life wrapped tightly around his neck. According to Dr. Garretson, Scott's face was swollen and purplish, as a result of strangulation: "The tongue itself was protruded well out of the mouth. The teeth were clenched over the tongue. In addition to that, there was what we call petechiae, which are . . . little hemorrhages on the skin which covered particularly the eyelids but also other parts of the face.

"The cloth was very, very tightly wound around the neck more than once. It was actually a pair of pajama bottoms. The legs were being used to wrap around the neck. The neck itself was very markedly indented, and the ridges of the cloth could be seen indenting the neck, compressing the windpipe of the trachea so the neck appeared abnormally thin as if the tissue had almost been removed from it. The neck itself was just extremely thin, much thinner than you would expect from a person of this size. . . . [B]ruises were actually continuous and went from the jaw down to above the collarbone . . . and all the way around the neck" (*People of the State of Illinois vs. Thomas Odle*, 1986).

Sean lay on his back with his head resting on Scott's right leg. The coroner testified that Sean "had perhaps the largest number of wounds. He had multiple wounds. Face, the back of the head, the neck, both on the right side and the left side. And in addition, [he] had several wounds over the lower anterior chest area just above the liver, and had some wounds on the back of his head.

"The wound in the front of his neck was a very large wound. It was somewhat V-shaped, perhaps three inches long and an inch and a half in height at the wide part of the V that . . . severed his windpipe and also cut across . . . the anterior portion of his esophagus.

"The wounds of the right side of the neck, none of which were fatal, didn't cut across any of the great vessels. . . . He had one stab wound on the left side of his neck, which again cut through the internal jugular vein. . . . And then another wound above that which cut through the body of one of his vertebrae and transected, or cut through, totally, the spinal cord at that level.

"He had two lethal wounds . . . the internal jugular vein on the left side of the neck which was cut across . . . and also the laceration of the spinal cord would have caused death. . . . [T]he wound of the spinal cord was probably the last wound received" (*People of the State of Illinois vs. Thomas Odle*, 1986).

Of fourteen-year-old Robyn Odle, the coroner noted that she "had a very large wound on the lower side of her back which had . . . perforated into the abdomen [and] was associated with very little bleeding. She had a series of wounds on the right side of her neck. The lower stab wound on the right side of her neck had cut across the internal jugular vein. And the upper stab wound of the right side of the neck had cut across and transected the right carotid artery. Either one of these two wounds would have been fatal" (*People of the State of Illinois vs. Thomas Odle*, 1986).

Absent from Robyn's pale face was the wide-eyed look of terror that the young girl almost certainly possessed when her older brother revealed the surprise he had promised her.

> Why? I have no clue. I just know I'd had enough. It's like this thing just chose me. I feel like it chose me, not me choosing it. Why this particular action took place, why I chose this day or this particular time, I don't know. It was like I was looking at myself, from the outside. It was me doing everything, but it wasn't me. It was like somebody else. Like it really wasn't happening. Like a dream or something. But it was real.
>
> I don't know why I had to do it. I had to. I just had to.

8

Arrest, Confession, and County Jail

Tom Odle would spend his last night as a free man in the Travel Inn Motel in Mt. Vernon. The warm and welcoming motel sign dominated the property. Rooms were accessed from the parking lot, and cars were parked in front of the room doors. That's where Tom parked his father's car, a brown, 1978 Mercury Marquis. The motel room's interior was typical of the time: dark flowered bedspreads, dark and slightly dusty curtains drawn on the only window. Opposite the front door, white light glowed in the bathroom. Room 125 would have reeked of marijuana.

After some investigation, police chief Ron Massey and sergeant William Degenhardt of the Mt. Vernon Police Department, together with special agent Charles Parker of the Illinois State Police Division of Criminal Investigation and detective Mike Anthis of the Jefferson County Sheriff's Department staked out room 125 from the Eagles Club parking lot directly across the street. They asked the motel owner to call room 125 and remind the guests that checkout time was 11:00 A.M. At 9:50 the morning of November 9, 1985, Tom Odle and a girl were seen leaving room 125. Agent Parker and detective Anthis immediately crossed the street in Parker's police car and blocked the exit of the '78 Mercury. Tom Odle was read his rights and arrested at 10:05.

> We got a phone call from the front desk that we had to check out, so we did. But before we left the room, I smoked a joint laced with the dust I had gotten the night before. Theresa didn't want any, so I smoked it all. On the way to the car the

police appeared with their guns pointing and yelling at me to freeze and demanding to know if I was Tom Odle.

To this day, I never thought that small town had that many guns to point at one person. They initially treated me with kid gloves, no rough handling, soft tones, and almost like they did not want to be doing it at all. But now I know it was because they didn't want to lose the case against me on some police brutality. I was patted down, handcuffed, and placed in the back of a squad car.

On Saturday, November 9, 1985, the front-page headline of the *Register-News*, the daily newspaper of Mt. Vernon, Illinois, read, "MASS MURDER HERE: Man in Custody after Five Family Members Slain." Greg Severin reported, "Five people were killed sometime Friday at 1005 S. 23rd St. and police are looking for an 18-year-old man in connection with the murder. State Police have issued a bulletin indicating that they are seeking Tom Odle, a member of the family, for questioning. Dead are Bob Odle and Carol L. Odle, each approximately 39, and their three children, Robyn, 14, Sean, 13, and Scott 10. A source close to the investigation, who asked not to be identified, said the five people were stabbed repeatedly. The bodies of the man, his wife and three children were discovered after 9:03 P.M. Friday by police when Bob Odle failed to show up for his 4 P.M.-to-midnight shift at Illinois Bell. . . . Stunned neighbors reported being shocked by Friday's multiple slaying" (1985, November 9).

Confession

I was starting to feel the dust and that unreal feeling again while riding in the back of the squad car. Theresa was transported to the police station in another car. We went to the police station and I was given a soda and some cigarettes. They asked me if I knew why I was there, but I didn't say anything. So, they asked me again and I asked them if it was about my house. They said, "Yes, it is." They brought in a tape recorder, read me my rights, and had me initial them. Then they turned on the tape player and re-read me my rights. Then, they turned off the tape recorder and told me I was going to tell them what happened. Then, they turned the tape recorder back on. While they were asking me questions it seemed as if I was outside myself. I heard myself telling them what happened, but it was not me inside my body. It was like

I was outside myself wondering what was going on, because I had been stopped from taking my own life.

It was like I was recalling something I had seen in a movie, except that I was in the movie. It was a really weird feeling I cannot describe to this day. I was still a bit high from the PCP I had smoked in the joint before I was arrested, so I'm sure that added to the feeling. I was amazed when I woke up that morning that I only had a few joints left, since I know I had purchased over a half ounce of weed, some PCP, and a little cocaine the night before.

The voices were echoing in my head and everything was in a wave-like state. I did my best to understand why I was there and what they wanted of me, so the statement came pouring out of me. I was ready to tell someone to get it out of my system; for verification that it was real or just a bad dream. To this day, I still think this is all a bad dream and I'm going to wake up and everything will be back to normal, as it was before the crime. Once I gave the statement, they asked me some questions.

Excerpt from Tom Odle's confession statement

ANTHIS: And you cut yourself? How did that happen?

ODLE: My hand slid off the handle.

ANTHIS: Describe the knife to me just a little bit? About how long is the blade?

ODLE: About five, six inches.

ANTHIS: Long? Is it a narrow blade or a wide blade?

ODLE: It has—it's like, you know the kind of knives that are used in movies like *Friday 13*, stuff like that.

ANTHIS: Uh huh.

ODLE: It's called a butcher knife.

ANTHIS: Kind of wide at the end and comes to a point at the other end.

ODLE: Yes. It's one just like that.

ANTHIS: What kind of handle did it have on it?

ODLE: A wooden handle. It was an old hickory knife.

ANTHIS: What do you mean, old hickory, is that the brand name of it or

ODLE: It's the brand name of it.

ANTHIS: Old Hickory.

PARKER: What did you do with the knife after you finished with it?

ODLE: I left it in the bedroom.

PARKER: Do you remember where?

ODLE: On the dresser.

PARKER: On the dresser?

ANTHIS: In your parents' bedroom.

ODLE: In my parents' bedroom.

PARKER: Tom, why did you do this?

ODLE: I had to.

ANTHIS: You can't tell us why you had to?

ODLE: I just had to . . . they bitched at me for every little thing I did. I look
   at them wrong. What are you looking at me like that for? Constantly
   jumping on my throat.

ANTHIS: I see.

ODLE: Constantly. Constantly pressuring me.

ANTHIS: When did that happen? That Thursday night or early in the day
   Thursday or

ODLE: A long time.

ANTHIS: Okay. Give me an idea of what's a long time. Like weeks?

ODLE: Years.   (*People v. Odle*, 1986)

> There was a part of me that just wanted to say I do not know.
> But there was also this sarcastic part of me that gave them
> what they wanted to hear, as far as details. I just made stuff
> up that made their eyes get large to try to give them the feel-
> ing that I was not someone to mess with. It gave me a sense
> of power, so to speak. It felt good. I didn't feel like a victim,
> anymore. And I understood a little of what my mother must
> have felt to have her children afraid of her. Now that I'm
> older I can see that she was scared and did what she did so
> she wouldn't feel like a victim. But a victim of what?

Excerpt from Tom Odle's confession statement

ANTHIS: Ah, okay, so then you really had a problem with mom and dad,
   basically. Why did you do it to the other ones?

ODLE: Because they couldn't be there too.

ANTHIS: They couldn't be there too. You mean they couldn't stay there by
   themselves or because there was nobody else to take care of them?

ODLE: There wasn't nobody else.

ANTHIS: Well, somebody—you've got uncles and stuff, don't you?

ODLE: I know, but see they would find them and they would run and tell.

ANTHIS: Oh, somebody would tell on you and then you'd get caught, is that what you're saying? So did you—did you just get up Friday morning at 9:30 and start this?

ODLE: I thought about it Thursday night.

ANTHIS: Did you think about it Thursday night? What did you think about it? How bad it would be or how you would do it or who you would do it to or what?

ODLE: How I would do it.

ANTHIS: Did you discuss, you know, did you—not discuss, but did you think about the different ways you could do it or just pick out one? Huh?

ODLE: Everybody else was easy, it was just dad I had to worry about.

ANTHIS: Why were the other ones going to be easy? No resistance or they would just give in or

ODLE: No resistance.

ANTHIS: And you—the way you thought about it on Thursday night, in which to stab them or to hurt was the same way that you did it on Friday. You didn't think one way and then change your mind on Friday?

ODLE: Oh, I thought of several ways.

ANTHIS: Which ways did you think of?

ODLE: Oh, I thought about strangling them, shooting them.

ANTHIS: Okay.

ODLE: But I had to do something that wouldn't make any noise.

ANTHIS: You have neighbors that live close to your house down there then where you live?

ODLE: Yeh.

ANTHIS: So you considered all the factors, didn't you?

ODLE: Yeh.   (*People v. Odle*, 1986)

So, they took the statement, taped it, and I signed some stuff they told me to sign. Then they took me to the jail, but on the way out of the police station I was told there were T.V. cameras there and I should walk fast and hold my head up or down. But they had me regardless of what I did. I saw loads of people all around the courthouse, like there was something going on. I couldn't believe all those people were there because of me. And for what reason were they there?

On Sunday, November 10, 1985, a front-page article of the *Southern Illinoisan*, a regional newspaper, reported that Coroner Richard Garretson stated, "At least four of the bodies had been moved from the kitchen or another part of the house and then just kind of stacked on available floor space. . . . They were lying in pools of blood. . . . It was apparent the kitchen had been cleaned up rather extensively. Towels were laid on the carpet, and he'd dragged the bodies across the carpet." Mt. Vernon police chief Massey told reporters, "Thomas Odle offered no resistance when arrested Saturday morning as he tried to leave a motel on the city's south side" (Staff, 1985a).

On Monday, November 11, an article in the *Southern Illinoisan* by reporter David Fox of the Associated Press noted, "Stunned friends, relatives and co-workers described a slain family as quiet, yet friendly and active in their community." Evelyn Eller, mother of Carolyn Odle and grandmother of Tom Odle and his siblings, was quoted as saying, "She's all I had. My whole family went. I've just got one grandson left." Coroner Garretson stated, "There was more blood than I've seen in my 25 years as a doctor, and I've seen my share of blood." Sarah Shields, a neighbor who lived directly across the street from the Odles, said, "I would call them a quiet family; they never neighbored with any of us." Additionally, it was noted that "residents of the family's tree-lined middle-class neighborhood gathered in shocked groups Saturday as police searched the home for evidence. . . . Mrs. Eller said her daughter was president of the Horace Mann Elementary School PTA, and coworkers described Robert Odle as devoted to his job and family" (Fox, 1985, November 11).

On Monday, November 11, in a front-page *Register-News* article, "In Slayings of Mt. Vernon Family 18-Year-Old in Jail without Bond," John Callarman reported, "The killings in the small frame house at 1005 S. 23rd St. may have begun as early as 9:30 A.M. Friday. And they continued until about 4:15 P.M. That's the time frame established by law enforcement authorities after Thomas V. Odle, 18, admitted killing his parents, two brothers and a sister, according to Police Chief Ron Massey.

"'He did give a statement,' Massey said. 'He did admit the killings. He gave a reason—it was a family dispute, a problem with his parents.

"'We can go one step further,' Massey said. 'This was an ongoing problem over months or years. . . .

"'A weapon was found,' Massey said. 'It is believed to be the murder weapon.' He described it as a large, hickory butcher knife with a wooden handle and said it was found in the bedroom, where four of the bodies were discovered. . . .

"Deputy Sheriff Mike Anthis and Division of Criminal Investigation Agent Charles Parker made the arrest at about 9:50 A.M. as Odle and a 15-year-old girl came out of Room 125 [of the Travel Inn Motel] and headed toward the car.

"Massey said Odle had picked up the girl sometime during the previous night, after driving around town for a while. They spent the night at the motel.

"Massey said the girl had no connection with the slayings and didn't know anything was wrong until she called friends Saturday morning and learned police were looking for Odle.

"Parker and Anthis questioned Odle for at least three hours following his arrest. Early Saturday afternoon, he was taken to the Jefferson County Jail, where he is being held without bond" (Callarman, 1985, November 11).

County Jail and the Media

I was processed in the jail, given a jumpsuit, and taken to the shower. I was told to put on the jumpsuit, but I still had those joints on me because they had never really searched me. So, I kept them on me and was given some bed linen along with some towels and stuff. I knew someone in jail already, who sent me some cigarettes, cosmetics, and a few candy bars. His mom even sent me some things like t-shirts, socks, and drawers.

I was listening to the news on some T.V. in the jail and they were talking about what had happened. I still did not believe it. I even asked to call my dad and the jailer laughed at me. I got mad at him and tried to hit him for laughing at me. A trustee came and told me that what I had heard on T.V. was about what I had done. But I was just not ready to believe something like that. I just laid down and went to sleep to try to get rid of the effects of the drugs, so I could think, because I couldn't keep a clear thought in my head.

When I got up, I noticed I was in jail and it took me a few seconds to gather in my surroundings. Then I realized that what I thought was a dream, was in fact, real. So, I talked to who I knew there and was told the same story that had been told to me earlier. I knew the trustee. Plus, I knew his brother. He used to ask me all kinds of questions and because I knew him, I would talk to him. After I had been there a few days, the officers brought me the statement I had made. After reading it, I concluded that what they were all saying was true. I even corrected the spelling of my siblings' names. It just had to be true because my signature was on the paper they showed me.

I had to wait until the weekend was over to go to court. In the meantime, I had all these Bible preachers at my cell door preaching at me. It was driving me crazy. I had to keep running them off by cussing them out because all I wanted was to be left alone to collect my thoughts and figure out what was going on and what was going to happen. I had to figure out once and for all if this was real or not. I could not think with all those people screaming that I was going to hell and to repent and on and on and on.

So, I finally went to court and there were T.V. cameras everywhere. That was just blowing my mind. They read the charges and I just started shaking and could not stop. I just wanted to die right then, just like I did when I woke up that morning and got a taste of what had happened. But I still could not believe what was happening.

On Monday, November 11, the *Register-News* listed the obituaries of Robert Odle, Carolyn Odle, Robyn Odle, Sean Odle, and Scott Odle. Robert, Robyn, Sean, and Scott Odle were preceded in death by Virgil Odle, Robert's father and the grandfather of Robyn, Sean, and Scott. It was also noted that all five deceased members of the Odle family were survived by Thomas Virgil Odle, who had received his middle name in honor of his grandfather (Staff, 1985b). The following are excerpts from the *Register-News* obituaries of the Odle family members:

Robert E. Odle, 39, 1005 S. 23rd St., died Friday at his home. . . . Mr. Odle was a mechanic for the Illinois Bell Telephone Co. . . . He is survived by one. . . .

Carolyn Louise Odle, 39, 1005 S. 23rd St., died Friday at her home. . . . Mrs. Odle was past president of the Horace Mann Parent-Teacher Organization and was a volunteer for the Horace Mann School library. . . . She is survived by one. . . .

Robyn Lynn Odle, 14, 1005 S. 23rd St., died Friday at her home. . . . She was a student at the Mt. Vernon Township High School. . . . She is survived by one. . . .

Sean Robert Odle, 13, 1005 S. 23rd St., died Friday at his home. . . . He was a pupil at the Casey Junior High School. . . . He is survived by one. . . .

Scott Jay Odle, 10, 1005, S. 23rd St., died Friday at his home. . . . He was a pupil at the Horace Mann School. . . . He is survived by one. . . . (Staff, 1985b)

On the front page of the November 12 *Southern Illinoisan*, a studio portrait of the Odle family taken approximately six months prior to the crime ran with an article on the killings. Reporter David Fox noted that "funeral services for the slain family were scheduled for this morning at Park Avenue Baptist Church" (1985, November 12).

The next day, five days after the murders, "Odle Formally Charged with Five Murders," a front-page article of the *Register-News*, related, "Thomas V. Odle mumbled 'Yes, sir,' five times as Circuit Judge Donald E. Garrison asked the 18-year-old if he understood each of the five counts of murder filed against him.

"Odle shook slightly and continuously as he sat alone at the defendant's table in Circuit Court here Tuesday afternoon as he was formally charged with murdering the other members of his immediate family.

"State's Attorney Kathleen Alling, in a news conference following the proceedings, said there is no evidence to indicate the five slayings related to drug use or drug abuse. 'I don't think we have any evidence that indicates that this was a crime that was prompted by drug use or drug abuse,' she told reporters.

"Some of Odle's relatives and friends had indicated to reporters that the suspect had a drug problem, and the minister at the funeral of the five family members emphasized the importance of solving the drug problem here. . . .

"Alling said it was too soon to determine if she would ask for the death penalty in the case. She said she is still waiting to learn if insanity is a factor, the family background and all the evidence in the case. 'Certainly, the factors are there,' she said, referring to the legal requirements for the death penalty.

"Those requirements spelled out by Garrison include the defendant's age—at least 17 on the date the crime was committed, more than one victim, or death resulting from exceptionally brutal or heinous behavior indicative of wanton cruelty. . . .

"Alling and assistant State's Attorney Rob Crego said the suspect left the house and picked up two of the children at school before they were slain Friday afternoon. . . . 'We do have evidence that he did leave the house and did pick up the children from school,' Alling added. Neither would speculate on the order of the killings, but Alling said, 'It is our feeling it's premeditated.'

"She declined to comment on the motive, other than to say, 'What we have so far is that there was a family disagreement on an ongoing basis over more than one or two weeks'" (Staff, 1985, November 13).

On the same date, a *Southern Illinoisan* story quoted Jefferson County sheriff Bob Pitchford: "He admitted killing them; he signed a confession. He said he had no feelings or remorse, no remorse about it at all" (Staff, 1985, November 13b).

In another piece about the Odle family funeral in the *Register-News* on November 13, Meta Minton and Randy Snyder reported, "About 400 relatives, friends and curiosity-seekers attended the funeral for members of the slain Odle family Tuesday—the same day their accused killer, eldest son Thomas V. Odle, 18, was making his first appearance in circuit court in Jefferson County Court house on five counts of murder. . . .

"Five hearses carried the bodies of Robert and Carolyn Odle, both 39, daughter Robyn, 14, and sons Sean, 13, and Scott, 10, from a closed-casket ceremony at Park Avenue Baptist Church to Memorial Gardens Cemetery, where they were interred at the family plot near the main entrance" (Minton & Snyder, 1985, November 13).

Reverend Gary Fore addressed the mourners during the graveside service: "'Certainly the community feels bitterness and anger. . . . But we desperately need to avoid that anger because it is destructive to us and destructive to those around us. . . . The amount of pain you have right now is a measure of the depth of love you had for these people. If one child passes through here and figures alcohol and drugs are really not the fun they figured them to be, that they're really not worth it compared to the pain they bring. . . . If one parent passes through here and realizes that choosing up sides and being abusive to each other in the family is not healthy . . . then these have not died in vain. . . . One of the hardest things in losing a loved one is why? We want to know. There are things going on that we don't understand right now and we can't'" (Minton & Snyder, 1985, November 13).

An editorial in the *Register-News* on November 13, 1985, said, "At least seven television stations, two wire services, numerous out-of-town newspapers and countless radio stations sent reporters to Mt. Vernon to cover the mass murder of the Odle family here" (Staff, 1985, November 13a).

A front-page story of the *Register-News* on Friday, November 22, 1985, reported, "Eighteen-year-old Thomas V. Odle, in an earlier-than-scheduled court appearance, pleaded innocent in Circuit Court here Thursday to five counts of murder in the death of his parents, two brothers and a sister." His attorney, public defender James Henson, had reportedly advised his client to waive the right to a preliminary hearing because the testimony of law-enforcement officers, specifically involving detailed descriptions of the crime scene, would have a damaging effect on the defense. Assistant public defender Charl Stowe was appointed co-counsel. Circuit judge Lehman D. Krause, in response to state's attorney Alling's motion, ordered Odle to undergo a psychiatric examination (Staff, 1985, November 22).

On the same date, Steve Allen of Mt. Vernon, in a *Register-News* letter to the editor, commented, "There were six members of a Mt. Vernon family whose lives were lost: Tom Odle was also a fatality. The toughest thing for us to grasp is that what Tom Odle did was not the problem, but a reaction to the problem. I believe when all the facts are in, we will find out that the things that were wrong in Tom Odle's life didn't just occur recently, but were a culmination of problems piling up over a long period of time. There were warning signs apparently that something was wrong, because his grandmother, Mrs. Eller, was quoted as saying: 'Tommy' had been sent to the service because 'they thought it might straighten him out, but it didn't.' How tragic, when we expect the schools or the military to solve or make up for what is lacking or not right at home" (Allen, 1985).

Psychiatric and Psychological Examinations

A little over three weeks after the crime, on December 2, 1985, Tom Odle underwent a court-ordered forensic psychological evaluation by Carolyn Weyand, PhD. She determined that Tom manifested chronic depression of mild to moderate severity that was due to a pervasive sense of loneliness and emptiness associated with feelings of fear, anger, and desperation. She concluded that he seemed to view the world "as a dangerous, hostile place. Those who are responsible for giving care and protection are perceived as indifferent, cold, or absent. Tom relates to the world at a primitive 'eat or be eaten' level. . . . Tom has failed to develop mature restraints or the ability to redirect primitive urges into productive channels." The psychologist concluded that "there was a striking absence of guilt or remorse, especially considering Tom's current situation" (*People v. Odle*, 1986).

The Thematic Apperception Test (TAT), a projective psychological instrument, was administered by Dr. Weyand to Tom to assess personality and psychopathology in a structured format. The TAT consists of a series of black-and-white pictures depicting ambiguous social scenes. The examinee is required to interpret the pictures by telling a story about what the pictures represent to him or her. Ostensibly, the stories reveal unconscious motives, internal conflicts, and repressed feelings that the examinee is otherwise unable to articulate. In response to a picture of the black silhouette of a male figure reaching through an open window framed against a solid black background, Tom responded, "'This looks like me . . . gazing out the window letting my imagination run . . . thinking of old memories . . . having some trouble sorting things out. He might be a thief in the night escaping out the window. He feels depressed-lonely, looking for friend to talk to, can't find no one . . . left to sort things out by himself. I like this picture'" (*People v. Odle*, 1986).

Tom also underwent a court-ordered forensic psychiatric examination by Lawrence L. Jeckel, MD, on December 2, 1985. Based on his review of records from the DCFS, Dr. Jeckel documented, "Mrs. Odle had a propensity for rigid and sadistic treatment of the boy and Mr. Odle protected his wife." Similar to the abuse of Sean, Tom said he "was chained to his bed as a young boy for 'two or three years' because he would 'break into people's houses at night.'" He added, "The father was 'just a bystander' while mother beat the children" (*People v. Odle*, 1986).

"Thomas said he had thought about hurting his family before," Dr. Jeckel reported. "He decided that he would kill his family the night prior to the alleged crime when father and mother told him he had to leave the home." He added, "Thomas told me he still could not believe he had hurt his family. He told me, 'I don't think I have a conscience. I don't feel guilty about what I done.' He still called the house and found it hard to believe that his parents were not there." Additionally, "he said one reason he killed the entire family was because he 'did not want them hurt by mother's death. . . . My mother was the one I really wanted; she mentally abused me.' He described past abuse, such as 'being beaten by my mother with a belt all over my body, and when I was 10 she smashed my thumb with a hammer. My mother said I was no good and wouldn't be anything'" (*People v. Odle*, 1986).

Dr. Jeckel concluded, "Thomas has a severe, chronic chaotic personality style which has object and self-destructive features. He grew up with little structure and love. He suffers from a pervasive sense of being out of control. . . . The trigger for the alleged crimes was his ejection from the family home. Thomas saw this ejection as the final abandonment by his family and the ultimate abuse." Dr. Jeckel diagnosed Tom with antisocial personality disorder and opined that he was fit to stand trial and had been able to appreciate the criminality of his actions at the time of the crime. The diagnostic criteria for antisocial personality disorder are provided in table 3 at the end of this chapter.

On December 9, 1985, one week after Dr. Jeckel's court-ordered psychiatric examination, Tom Odle was transported from Mt. Vernon to the Cook County Jail in Chicago, where he underwent a forensic psychiatric examination by defense expert Henry G. Conroe, MD. Dr. Conroe noted, "His affect was generally bland and his mood was mildly depressed and anxious. He began crying when speaking of feeling he should have kept his youngest brother, Scott, alive." After recounting the events of the day before the killings, Tom described in detail the manner in which each of his family members was killed (*People v. Odle*, 1986).

When asked to describe his relationship with his mother, Tom stated that there were "'two sides to her.' One side was 'allright.'" Her other side was "'very, very violent.' She would throw anything that was available or slap the children. 'She didn't know when to quit with the belt.' She often argued with her husband about the punishment. 'She always yelled and screamed, and we would always end up both screaming.'"

The psychiatrist noted that Tom "described chronic feelings of hope-lessness and depression. He had suicidal thoughts of shooting himself in the head. He spoke of feeling remorseful but also being relieved." Dr. Con-roe diagnosed him with borderline personality disorder with antisocial

Antisocial Personality Disorder versus Borderline Personality Disorder

Table 3. Diagnostic criteria for antisocial personality disorder

A. There is a pervasive pattern of disregard for and violation of the rights of others occurring since age fifteen years, as indicated by three (or more) of the following:
1. *Failure to conform to social norms with respect to lawful behaviors as indicated by repeatedly performing acts that are grounds for arrest*
2. *Deceitfulness, as indicated by repeated lying, use of aliases, or conning others for personal profit or pleasure*
3. *Impulsivity or failure to plan ahead*
4. *Irritability and aggressiveness, as indicated by repeated physical fights or assaults*
5. *Reckless disregard for safety of self or others*
6. *Consistent irresponsibility, as indicated by repeated failure to sustain consistent work behavior or honor financial obligations*
7. *Lack of remorse, as indicated by being indifferent to or rationalizing having hurt, mistreated, or stolen from another*

B. The individual is at least age eighteen years.
C. There is evidence of conduct disorder with onset before age fifteen years.
D. The occurrence of antisocial behavior is not exclusively during the course of schizophrenia or a manic episode.

SOURCE: Adapted from *Diagnostic and statistical manual of mental disorders*, American Psychiatric Association, 2000, Washington, DC: APA, pp. 701–706.

features, based on his "impulsivity, his pattern of unstable and intense interpersonal relationships, his lack of control of anger, his frequent mood shifts, and his intolerance for being alone" (*People v. Odle*, 1986).

Dr. Conroe concluded that Tom's behavior was a symptom of a "malignant family system." He opined, "His mother's coldness and sadism and his father's unavailability and passivity led to Tom's difficulties controlling his anger and his impulsivity. Tom's indifference toward the lives of his family members was similar to his mother's attitude. His upbringing led to his having a serious mental disease, a Borderline Personality Disorder with Anti-social features. This mental disorder was present on November 8, 1985, and his behavior on that day was clearly an outcome of his being a member of this highly disturbed family where sadism and indifference were the norm." The diagnostic criteria for borderline personality disorder are provided in table 4 at the end of this chapter.

Table 4. Diagnostic criteria for borderline personality disorder

A pervasive pattern of instability of interpersonal relationships, self-image, and affects, and marked impulsivity beginning by early adulthood and present in a variety of contexts, as indicated by five (or more) of the following:

1. *Frantic efforts to avoid real or imagined abandonment.*
2. *A pattern of unstable and intense interpersonal relationships characterized by alternating between extremes of idealization and devaluation*
3. *Identity disturbance: Markedly and persistently unstable self-image or sense of self*
4. *Impulsivity in at least two areas that are potentially self-damaging (e.g., spending, sex, substance abuse, reckless driving, binge eating)*
5. *Recurrent suicidal behavior, gestures, or threats, or self-mutilating behavior*
6. *Affective instability due to a marked reactivity of mood (e.g., intense episodic dysphoria, irritability, or anxiety usually lasting a few hours and only rarely more than a few days)*
7. *Chronic feelings of emptiness*
8. *Inappropriate, intense anger or difficulty controlling anger (e.g., frequent displays of temper, constant anger, recurrent physical fights)*
9. *Transient, stress-related paranoid ideation or severe dissociative symptoms*

SOURCE: Adapted from *Diagnostic and statistical manual of mental disorders*, American Psychiatric Association, 2000, Washington, DC: APA, pp. 706–710.

9

On Trial for Life

The next phase of Tom Odle's life would unfold in a series of courtrooms. Following a coroner's inquest, the pretrial hearings took place in the Jefferson County Courthouse, in Mt. Vernon, the county seat, from December 1985 through February 1986. The trial, however, was moved to Richland County in response to a change-of-venue motion by the defense, who held that a fair trial in Jefferson County would not be possible due to the publicity the crime and the defendant had received.

Pretrial Hearings

On November 26, 1985, a little over two weeks following the murders, the deaths of the five Odle family members were ruled homicides at a coroner's inquest. Dr. Richard Garretson, Jefferson County coroner, testified on the state's behalf. Garretson distributed photos of the victims to the jurors and gave his account of the crime scene, victim by victim and wound by wound. When assistant state's attorney Kathleen Alling asked him to characterize the wounds and relate them to the victims' deaths, Garretson testified, "I would say they would be quite painful; and in addition to that, it's a suffocation death even though we call it immediate on the coroner's death certificate. It takes minutes for somebody to die. That would be a very agonizing death" (*People v. Odle*, 1986).

Pathologist James R. Miller, MD, who had conducted the autopsies on all five of the victims, also testified for the state, concluding that a "considerable amount of force would be required to inflict those wounds" (*People v. Odle*, 1986).

The six-member coroner's jury reached a verdict after approximately twenty minutes of deliberation.

> I was assigned two attorneys; one I hardly ever saw and one I saw all the time. The one I saw frequently would tell me that I would walk and not to worry about a thing. I was young. The legal system was something I left to the lawyers, as I had done once before. He told me this and that was going to happen, so I believed him. There was never a doubt that I would walk after we had the trial. He took it upon himself to take care of issues regarding the estate. I didn't know what was going on, and I didn't know he was doing that until the State brought it up in a motion at a hearing one day. But again, I just left it alone because he was the lawyer. He told me not to worry, and he said that I would walk out of the courthouse right after the trial. So, I never worried one bit. I was in a cellblock with a good friend of mine who was there 90 percent of the time I was there. So, my pre-trial time went really smooth and fast. There were no problems from me, and I saw my attorney almost every night. So, there were no worries on my part.
>
> People wrote me letters, especially girls and women wanting to be my friend and congratulating me on doing something that they had only thought about doing because they were mistreated and abused, also. There was also some kind of fan club for me. Kids were threatening their parents to do to them what I had done to mine if they didn't leave them alone. It was crazy. I liked the attention I was getting, and I even reconnected with an old friend I had a crush on for years. She wrote to me, so I wrote back, and we found each other in a new light. And I had the Christians beating down my door and everything else. It was crazy.
>
> I had to see several doctors during that time, but I didn't really know what to say to them. With some of them I was very careful because I didn't want to sound crazy. With others I just answered questions the way I was told to answer them. I still had my pride to think of, and I did not want to be crazy. However, I know now that it might have saved me. But I was not going to give in. I guess there was a part of me that was finally getting attention, and I was enjoying

the recognition. Obviously, that was not the right way to go about it, but for once in my life I could be me without someone lurking to tear me down or shame me in front of other people. It was as if I had wings that were finally out and being used. I finally felt that I was becoming who I was supposed to be. It's bad for me to say it now, but that's how I felt inside at that time.

During the January 31, 1986, pretrial hearing for the defense motion to suppress Tom's confession due to his drug-induced, altered mental state when he was arrested, the court would get an early but lasting impression of the character of Tom Odle. The impression of an immature and defiant boy who showed little remorse for his actions would influence the court, the prosecutors, and the press throughout the legal proceedings to follow.

The pretrial hearing was the only time Tom testified on his own behalf. The questions focused on his drug use on the night of the crimes and at other times. He talked about the hallucinogenic effects he was experiencing from the angel dust (PCP) he smoked just before he was arrested. The prosecution was eager to confirm that Tom was lucid enough to understand what he had done and that he understood his rights when they were read to him. In the end, Tom managed to portray himself as a regular, knowledgeable drug user who had the presence of mind to stand trial for the crimes for which he was accused.

Excerpts from Assistant Public Defender Henson's Direct Examination

Q. Okay. Then in the morning before you left the motel, did you have any alcohol or drugs?

A. Yes.

Q. And what did you have in the morning?

A. In the morning I had a joint laced with dust.

. . . .

Q. So at the time that you were arrested, were you feeling any effects of alcohol or drugs or anything at that time?

A. I was just starting to.

. . . .

Q. Okay. How were you feeling at the time that the tape recorder was turned on? Do you recall?

A. Well, I was pretty high. I was just kind of watching the wave—the walls wave. I remember mumbling, talking and stuff like that.

. . . .

Q. And do you feel that—that everything that you stated there was the truth?

A. I wouldn't go as far as to say everything I said was the truth.

Q. Do you know?

A. Well, from today, I can tell you that not all of it's the truth.

Q. Do you know why you would have told them something that wasn't the truth on that day?

A. Mixed up. Confused.

Q. And you remember the tape being stopped at the end?

A. Yeah.

Q. How did you feel at that time?

A. Lonely. Depressed.

. . . .

Q. Now, couple days later, I believe that they stated that they came and saw you in jail. Do you remember that?

A. Yes.

Q. Okay. Were you high at that time?

A. No.

Q. Do you recall them reading your rights to you at that time?

A. Yes.

Q. Okay. Did you sign your rights then?

A. Yes.

Q. Now, I'll show you the State's Exhibit #2. This is a copy of something. Would you take a look at that? Have you seen that before?

A. Yes.

Q. Is your signature on there?

A. Yes.

Q. Do you recall seeing it at the—on that time and— and signing it on the 11th?

A. Yes.

Q. Did you—did you—did your—did you read the statement when they gave it to you?

A. Yes.

Q. Did you sign the statement?

A. Yes.

Q. Did you sign it because it was a true and accurate statement?

A. Not really.

Q. Why did you sign it?

A. Just to get it over with.   (*People v. Odle*, 1986)

Excerpts from ASA Robert Crego's Cross-Examination

Q. What is angel dust?

A. PCP.

Q. What's PCP?

A. It's a hallucinogenic drug.

Q. Is it an animal tranquilizer?

A. I wouldn't say so.

Q. You'd say it's like LSD?

A. Yes.

Q. What does it make you do when you take it?

A. Well, to me it just makes me feel real good.

Q. Well, the morning of—of the 9th, when you went to the police station, you said that you were hearing things, just like a bunch of words run together. Are you hearing things like that right now?

A. No.

Q. You can hear the questions I'm asking you and you can answer them; can't you?

A. Yeah.

Q. And you had the opportunity to hear a tape in the back room here just a few—few minutes ago and it had your voice on it; did it not?

A. Yes.

Q. And you were asked questions by police officers at that time; were you not?

A. Yes.

Q. And you answered the questions; did you not?

A. Yes.

Q. Are the walls waving right now as you sit here?

A. No.

Q. They were waving then though; weren't they?

A. Yeah.

Q. Did you tell anybody that the walls were waving right then though?

A. No.

Q. Why not?

A. 'Cause I didn't feel like it.

. . . .

Q. Did you feel it was hallucination that you were at the police station?

A. In a way, but I knew it was real, though.

Q. You're saying that you knew it was real, but in a way you felt like it was a hallucination?

A. Yeah.   (*People vs. Odle*, 1986)

Mental Status

Following Tom's testimony and arguments of counsel, Judge Donald E. Garrison promptly denied the defense motion to suppress Tom's statement of confession. During the pretrial hearings, which ultimately resulted in the trial's relocation to Richland County, the reports of the forensic examiners who had evaluated Tom following the murders were submitted into evidence. The report of forensic psychiatrist Lawrence L. Jeckel, MD, documented the following:

> In reviewing the historical data, of great importance are the considerable conflicts in the family prior to this incident. DCFS previously investigated the parents' treatment of a younger brother, Sean. He was chained to his bed for one to two years because he would steal food at night. At one point, Sean was placed in DCFS custody. DCFS notes reflect a chaotic family structure with poor parenting skills. Mrs. Odle had a propensity for rigid and sadistic treatment of the boy and Mr. Odle protected his wife. However, the family pursued the recommended treatment by DCFS and cooperated in the investigation.

. . . .

> Thomas said he, too, was chained to his bed as a young boy for "two or three years" because he would break into people's houses at night. He said his mother told him he had "newborn fever," and a skull fracture when he was little. Thomas denied his father ever beat him or any of the other children. The father was "just a bystander" while mother beat the children.

. . . .

> Thomas said he had thought about hurting his family before. He decided he would kill his family the night prior to the alleged crime when father and mother told him he had to leave the home. . . . He said "getting high made me feel good and I felt like I had more control." In the past, he had used a variety of street drugs including LSD, amphetamines, barbiturates, PCP, and cocaine in addition to marijuana.

. . . .

> Thomas told me he still could not believe he had hurt his family. He told me, "I don't think I have a conscience. I don't feel guilty about what I done." He still called the house and found it hard to believe

that his parents were not there. . . . He said one reason he killed the entire family was because he "did not want them hurt by mother's death." To quote Thomas further, "my mother was the one I really wanted; she mentally abused me." He described past abuse, such as "being beaten by my mother with a belt all over my body, and when I was 10 she smashed my thumb with a hammer. My mother said I was no good and wouldn't be anything. My mother always hurt my little brother, and father never stopped her."

. . . .

Thomas has a severe, chronic chaotic personality style which has object and self-destructive features. He grew up with little structure and love. He suffers from a pervasive sense of being out of control. . . . The trigger for the alleged crimes was his ejection from the family home. Thomas saw this ejection as the final abandonment by his family and the ultimate abuse.

. . . .

I believe he is able to cooperate in his own defense and is fit to stand trial. I detected no evidence which would indicate a mental disease or defect. Antisocial personality disorder is a long-standing personality style rather than a specific illness. Thomas was able to appreciate the wrongfulness of the alleged crime and conform his conduct to standards of the law. (*People v. Odle*, 1986)

The report of forensic psychiatrist and defense expert Henry G. Conroe, MD, SC, provides a lengthy, detailed description of the events leading up to and surrounding the day of the crime, the long-standing abuse by Tom's mother, and Tom's chronic drug abuse. After that, Conroe focused on Tom's current mental state.

He described chronic feelings of hopelessness and depression. He had suicidal thoughts of shooting himself in the head. He spoke of being remorseful, but also being relieved because, "I will never hear them bitching, putting me down." At this point, he sees no future for himself. But he denied current suicidal ideation.

. . . .

[T]here is evidence of Tom Odle having two psychiatric diagnoses. The first is Borderline Personality with Anti-social features as seen in Tom's impulsivity, his pattern of unstable and intense interpersonal relationships, his lack of control of anger, his frequent mood shifts, and his intolerance of being alone. The second diagnosis is mixed substance abuse as indicated by his past history.

While Dr. Conroe agreed with most of Dr. Jeckel's findings and opinions, he disagreed with the latter's conclusions regarding DCFS interventions.

Dr. Jeckel's statement that "the family pursued the recommended treatment by DCFS and cooperated in the investigation" was erroneous. For example, a letter from 7/13/81 to DCFS described the unwillingness of the family to accept therapeutic services. In addition, Mr. Odle balked at paying $170 per month for Sean's support in 1983 despite an income of $30,000 per year.

. . . .

Sean's situation was a symptom of a malignant family system. Tom's behavior was another symptom of this malignancy. He was also the focus of physical and emotional abuse. . . . Tom's indifference towards the lives of his family members was similar to his mother's attitude. His upbringing led to his having a serious mental disease, a Borderline Personality Disorder with Anti-social features. (*People v. Odle*, 1986)

On April 9, 1986, one month before Tom's trial was scheduled to begin, Michael E. Althoff, PhD, a defense expert, conducted another psychological evaluation of Tom. Althoff agreed with Dr. Conroe's double diagnoses. In his conclusion, Althoff summarizes the case and Tom's mental state on the day of the crimes.

There is a longstanding, documented history of physical and emotional abuse occurring toward Sean and, to a lesser extent, toward Tom. The fact that this is documented, especially regarding Sean, increases the likelihood that this kind of behavior occurred toward the other children. There is significant evidence that suggests Tom suffered from chronic feelings of estrangement and alienation from his family. The history of unsuccessful emancipation from his family suggests a very hostile and dependent relationship.

. . . .

Given the above personality traits and family dynamics, the following represents a scenario by which this examiner most usefully understands the instant offenses. Tom developed into a damaged, alienated and ambivalent individual with severe problems in controlling his impulses and, as a late adolescent, experienced additional rejection outside of the family.

. . . .

This ultimate rejection and potential separation from his family in combination with the effects of the marijuana and alcohol, along with intense underlying anger and feelings of estrangements, allowed these acts to be initiated. The temporal disintegration and depersonalization effects created a feeling of self-estrangement and unreality that lessened concern for future consequences and his ambivalence toward loss of control. This, in turn, resulted in the initiation of the first homicide. The unleashing of this act of vengeance toward the figure of paramount importance in his family built the foundation for the initiation of the remaining homicides. Having killed his father who was ostensibly the protector of the family allowed him to assume the role of avenger and take the power which his father never consistently exercised. In some sense at this point he likely identified with his father. The remaining homicides can most usefully be understood as the acting out of this "caretaking" role. At one level, Tom finally solved the familial conflict and difficulties through the remaining homicides. (*People v. Odle*, 1986)

Among the psychological tests Althoff administered were some projective drawings (see Draw-a-Family Test, illustrations gallery). The psychologist's interpretation of Tom's drawing of his dead family members includes the following:

His associations in response to a request to draw a picture of his family prior to their deaths suggest significant familial alienation and estrangement. When asked to initiate the task, he asked, "do you want me included, too?" When given the choice of whether to include himself or not, he excluded himself. . . . The drawings suggest perceptions of maternal figures as being critical and disappointing. The figure of the father was drawn first indicating that this figure is likely most impressive or important to Tom. The figure of his brother Sean was drawn last, suggesting that Sean is likely viewed as least important in Tom's life. The absence of a drawing of himself suggests significant feelings of being inconsequential, powerless and emotionally separate from the family unit. (*People v. Odle*, 1986)

The Trial

The Richland County Courthouse, a three-story limestone structure with stately columns framing the entrance, sits in the town square of Olney, Illinois, the county seat, having risen from the ashes of the previous courthouse that burned in 1909. For Tom Odle, the oak-paneled courtroom within the Second Judicial Circuit Court of Illinois would be the stage from which the Jefferson County state's attorney would present the evidence and witness testimony to Judge Garrison and a jury composed of locals from the small towns and farms in rural Southern Illinois.

Tom, shackled and wearing a standard, county-issued, orange jumpsuit, sat at a front table with his attorneys, public defenders James Henson and Charl Stowe. Prosecutors Kathleen Alling and Robert Crego, representing the State of Illinois, sat at a nearby table. The wooden chairs in the gallery behind Tom were filled. The rest of the standing-room-only crowd huddled at the back of the room. Reporters scribbled in notebooks and strained to get a view of the defendant and the string of witnesses.

They wouldn't see much reaction from Tom Odle. He sat still in his chair, his face blank, as though he still had not quite figured out why he was in the courtroom. The judge would read his blank stare as emotionless and without remorse.

> The trial was moved to another county because of all the publicity I was getting in my own county. During the stay at the new county jail, my cell was a single cell with no T.V. And, it was right behind a bar. I didn't know what to think about the whole situation, except that I was closer to going home, according to my attorney. He [Stowe] was still telling me that I was going to walk and that I would go home after the trial. So, naturally I was looking forward to the trial and going home. He would come and see me every morning.
>
> During the time that my life was on trial I did some stupid things. I laughed while people were testifying. I listened to so-called friends make stuff up against me just to get attention in what had become the three ring circus of my life. But I also saw people I barely knew step up and say good things about me and stand by me for a long period of time. And, I met some new people along the way. Some had my best interests at heart and others were just weirdoes who wanted information on how to join my fan club.

On Monday, May 12, 1986, the murder trial of Tom Odle began in the Richland County Courthouse in the little town of Olney, Illinois. A jury of six men and six women was selected from the jury pool. The prosecution called twenty-six witnesses to testify during the first three days of the trial. On day 3 of the trial, Tom's tape-recorded statement of confession was played in open court. The emotional impact of the graphic and detailed description of the killings, as told by the defendant, was evident on the faces of all who heard it.

One of the first trial witnesses was fifteen-year-old Theresa Blevins, who testified for the state and reiterated her pretrial-hearing testimony about what happened before and after the crimes. She said she first saw Tom at noon that day at Mt. Vernon High School; he was driving his father's car: "I asked him if he was still going to pick me up after school. And then he said he couldn't because he was going to take his brothers and sister to their grandmother's house. . . . [T]hat's about the time when I saw a speck of blood on, behind his left ear. And I told him and he looked in a mirror and licked it off with his finger." They made plans to get together that evening around 5:00 (*People v. Odle*, 1986).

Kim Cates and Larry Owens were already in Robert Odle's car when Tom picked Theresa up at 4:45.

Excerpt from Theresa Blevin's Testimony

BLEVINS: He had blood streaks from his wrist to his, to his elbow, on his
    right arm inside of it; and I assumed nothing.
ALLING: All right. Did you question him about it?
BLEVINS: No, I was intimidated to ask him any kind of question.
ALLING: Why was that?
BLEVINS: Because he gave me the impression that he never liked to be asked
    questions. And I was scared to.   (*People v. Odle*, 1986)

The four of them checked into the Travel Inn Motel at about 6 P.M. Tom rolled joint after joint and smoked most of them himself. Theresa said that after a while, "I was immune to it. I couldn't get high anymore." At about 9:30, Tom drove Larry and Kim home and returned to the motel, where he and Theresa spent the rest of the night.

In the morning, Theresa called a friend, Frances, as she described during her testimony:

BLEVINS: She told me that Tom was all over the news for killing some
    family. . . . I told her that I would go to the police station and

straighten it out. And I hung up the phone; and I said, "Tom, Frances says you're all over the news for killing some family." And his reaction was like, "really, wow." Then he wanted to talk to her. . . . He asked me to call Frances and he talked to her. But he really didn't say anything. He just said, "Yes," "No," "Really," you know, and he hung up.

ALLING: At that point, did you know whose family was dead, or just a family?

BLEVINS: She said "a family, some family." I didn't know. (*People v. Odle*, 1986)

Two days after the murders, Tom made a phone call to seventeen-year-old Cindy Blobaum, who also testified for the state. She explained that while they had dated at one time, they were just friends.

Excerpts from Cindy Blobaum's Testimony

BLOBAUM: He called and he said, "Hi little sis." And I said, "Who is this?" And he said, "Tom." I said, "Where are you at?" And he said, "Jail." And I said, "Oh." And I was quiet and I didn't say nothing. And he asked me how I was doing and I told him.

ALLING: Okay. Did you have further, how were you doing? What did you say?

BLOBAUM: I told him he shattered my brain.

ALLING: And what were you referring to?

BLOBAUM: He messed me up. I went into shock.

Tom called Blobaum two more times from jail. During the third call, he went into detail about each of the murders. But the attorneys were more interested in a conversation Blobaum had with Tom the Wednesday night before the murders. Tom visited her at a house where she was babysitting.

BLOBAUM: He asked me questions like what would I do if he wasn't around anymore.

ALLING: When he left that night, did he do anything unusual?

BLOBAUM: He said, "Cindy, I want you to make me proud of you," and then he gave me a big hug and left.   (*People v. Odle*, 1986)

Later, during the phone calls, Tom explained that he wanted to say good-bye without letting her know what he was going to do. From the prosecution's perspective, the time between the Wednesday visit and Friday's crimes spoke to premeditation.

Jeri Allyson Webb testified that she was on duty at the Travel Inn Motel on November 8, when Tom Odle checked in. Webb informed the court that he acted strangely and "he had devil's eyes." During the defense cross-examination, Webb was asked if Tom Odle still had devil's eyes while sitting in the courtroom. She acknowledged that she believed he did (*People v. Odle*, 1986).

The state rested its case after three days of prosecution witness testimony; the defense opened its case on Monday, May 19, 1986. Key defense witness, psychiatrist Dr. Conroe, testified that Tom manifested "borderline personality disorder with antisocial tendencies." As a result, Dr. Conroe testified, Tom "can slip into psychosis while at other times appear to function more normally." However, consistent with his opinion in the report of his December 9, 1985, examination of Tom, the psychiatrist stated that he was unable to determine if Tom was able to appreciate the criminality of his behavior or to conform his conduct to the requirements of the law at the time of the crime.

The following day, Tom's former girlfriend testified that she had undergone an abortion against his wishes and subsequently broke up with him after he returned from a short stint in the army: "I was young. I realized I wasn't ready to spend my life with just one person. . . . I guess he took it really hard" (*People v. Odle*, 1986).

On the fourth day of defense witness testimony, Althoff testified for more than seven hours. Based on the psychological evaluation he had conducted one month earlier, Dr. Althoff concurred with Dr. Conroe's opinion regarding the diagnosis of borderline personality disorder with antisocial tendencies. He stated that when Tom killed his father, "this in essence opened Pandora's Box—let out all the things in the darker side of his life." Althoff said that Tom's act of killing his father released years of suppressed hatred. In response to this emotional release, Tom then assumed the role of father and proceeded to kill his mother. After killing his mother, Tom then assumed the maternal role of disciplinarian, which resulted in the killing of his three siblings. Dr. Althoff concluded that although Tom was not in a psychotic state at the time of the murders, he was not mentally capable of appreciating the criminality of his actions at the time of the crime. He added that if Tom had not been apprehended by the police, he would have killed himself (*People v. Odle*, 1986).

On Friday, May 23, after five days of defense testimony, the defense rested without calling Tom Odle to testify on his own behalf.

On Tuesday, May 27, the state began and ended its rebuttal with the testimony of seven prosecution witnesses. Larry Johnson, a supervisor at the Illinois Department of Children and Family Services in Mt. Vernon, had been the supervisor on the Odle family case. He testified that during the thirty months DCFS handled the case, "there was no substantiation of abuse of Tom Odle." Regarding Sean, Johnson said, "[I]t was a physical abuse situation. There [were] two different perpetrators, both the parents and the brother. It was a situation in which Sean was abused over two different periods of time by the parents and one period of time by the brother that was substantiated. . . . We felt like Sean was the scapegoat of the family, that he was the object of the abuse of the parents."

Excerpt from Larry Johnson's Testimony

HENSON: Didn't you have information that Sean [had] . . . been chained to the bed on two different occasions?

JOHNSON: I believe the first occasion he was tied to the bed and the second occasion he was chained, was the allegation.

HENSON: Okay. And this had gone on for long periods of time, is that right?

JOHNSON: According to Sean, it had.

HENSON: And didn't you have information indicating that when Thomas Odle was younger that this had also happened to him?

JOHNSON: In December, 1983, Sean stated to his foster mother . . . that Tom had also been tied to [the] bed prior to Sean being tied to the bed.

(People v. Odle, 1986)

Jerry L. Boyd, PhD, a clinical psychologist, who had not actually examined Tom, also testified for the state. Dr. Boyd stated that the amount of marijuana and alcohol in Tom's system at the time of the crime would not make him violent. He also stated that a person with borderline personality disorder could "function less effectively" under the influence of those drugs but that it really depended on the person. The addition of angel dust to the mix, he admitted, could alter the user's perception of reality (*People v. Odle*, 1986).

Don Yearwood, who owned a body shop in Mt. Vernon and had hired Tom as a favor to Tom's father, also testified for the state. When asked about Tom's character, Yearwood said that Tom "was more or less lazy, he wouldn't really do the job he was assigned to do. And he—he was late coming to work and tried to leave early" (*People v. Odle*, 1986).

Joe Baldwin testified that he had also hired Tom, who "happened to be dating my daughter and he couldn't find a job and she convinced me that he needed one, so we hired him." He described Tom as lazy and dishonest. "When he was told to do things, he would just not do them, and at one point I confronted him and asked him, 'Did you lie about this?' And he said, 'Yes I lied'" (*People v. Odle*, 1986).

Dr. Jeckel, the last of sixty-four witnesses, testified for the state about his findings and opinions, based on the court-ordered psychiatric examination of Tom six months earlier. Jeckel reiterated his diagnosis of antisocial personality disorder and said that Tom's behavior was consistent with the diagnostic criteria of antisocial personality disorder, according to the *Diagnostic and Statistical Manual of Mental Disorders* of the American Psychiatric Association. While he stated that he did not have evidence that Tom manifested all the characteristics of antisocial personality disorder, he clearly had evidence of more than three of the characteristics necessary to meet the criteria for the diagnosis. He cited the following behaviors as representative of antisocial personality disorder: history of delinquency, persistent lying, repeated sexual intercourse in a casual relationship, repeated drunkenness or substance abuse, theft, vandalism, chronic violations of school or home rules, initiation of fights, and impulsivity. Jeckel countered the defense's claim that Tom had borderline personality disorder.

Excerpts from Dr. Jeckel's Testimony

JECKEL: I saw no evidence of what we call the mini-psychotic episodes, which can be a part of borderline personality disorder.

ALLING: You saw no evidence.

JECKEL: I saw no evidence. I did see evidence of homicidal thought that he had talked about killing others. I think there was a boyfriend of a girl he dated. I think someone had said that he'd talked about killing—perhaps being so mad to kill his parents. So, we did have evidence of that.

ALLING: That is not psychotic.

JECKEL: That is not psychotic.

ALLING: Did he have homicidal ideation the day before he committed the murders?

JECKEL: Yes.

ALLING: And on the day of the murder?

JECKEL: Yes, his comment was "My mother was the one I really wanted."

Dr. Jeckel also testified, "I don't see that he planned it for any period of time other than the night before that he—when the parents decided they were going to kick Tom Odle out once and for all did I see that the—you know, he intended to kill them." As such, according to Dr. Jeckel, the element of premeditation was very brief in contrast to the chronic abuse that Tom and his brother had suffered.

ALLING: Did you take into account the fact that Tom may have been abused by his parents?

JECKEL: Very much so.

ALLING: Would the fact that someone may have been an abused child necessarily make them mentally ill?

JECKEL: It can. I believe if you're persistently abused over a long period of time [it] can be very detrimental to your mental health.

ALLING: And with this in mind, did you take into account the fact that Tom was abused?

JECKEL: Yes.

ALLING: And still you came up with the fact that he was what?

JECKEL: That he had an anti-social personality disorder.

ALLING: Is that a mental disease or defect?

JECKEL: No, it's a pattern of behavior and thinking.

ALLING: So, you did not come to the conclusion that Tom was one of those abused children that are mentally ill.

JECKEL: I believe that the pattern of behavior, the anti-social personality disorder, may have had some cause by his abusive treatment and the family home situation, especially, you know, the sadistic treatment of his mother on—on Tom, and also, it—it appeared in another child, Sean, the sadistic behavior. . . . Because I think that sadistic behavior has such a damaging effect on children, and that in this family situation, mother was protected by the father, and I believe that—that—the homicidal impulses that Tom had can be attributed in part, in part, only in part, to the way he was treated by his mother.

. . . .

ALLING: Then, would you summarize what your findings were about Tom Odle?

JECKEL: I believe that Tom Odle did not have a mental disease or defect that would cause him to not appreciate the wrongfulness of his crime nor conform his conduct to the standards of the law.

(*People v. Odle*, 1986)

On Thursday, May 29, after all the testimony was in, the jury deliberated less than two hours before delivering their verdict to the court. Thomas

V. Odle was found guilty on five counts of murder in the first degree. The following day, Tom made his first statement in open court: "Your honor, I would like to right now waive my right to a jury sentence." The die for sentencing had been cast. It now was clear that Tom's life lay singularly in the hands of Judge Garrison, who ruled that the case be transferred back to Jefferson County for sentencing on June 30, 1986. Due to aggravating factors, including the killing of more than one person and the murder of a child under the age of twelve (Scott Odle), Tom was eligible to receive a death sentence.

> When I was found guilty, I had no real emotion. I wasn't really concerned about being found guilty. I was really pissed off at Stowe for leading me to believe I would walk out the door a free man. I had been led to believe I was going home. So, I was just waiting to go home.

The Sentencing Hearing

Thirteen witnesses were examined by the prosecution and the defense to assist the court in making a decision regarding the nature of Tom's sentence. It was made clear to all involved that the death penalty was most definitely on the table.

Yvonne Sexton, Carolyn Odle's best friend, was the first to take the stand. She testified that Tom stole a collection of bicentennial quarters from a filing cabinet that belonged to his dad. She said he also stole fifteen silver dollars that belonged to his mother and lunch money from his sister, Robyn. Sexton also related a story in which Tom stole a knife from a neighbor's house and that he had prompted Sean and Scott to steal money from purses out of parked cars at the Logan Street Church.

The next line of questioning for Sexton was to establish that Tom had been violent with members of his family. She recalled, "Tommy was chasing Sean through the house and he had pulled a knife on him. . . . I was told that Tom was not allowed to go to his grandmother's because he had struck her." When asked about violence aimed at Carolyn, Sexton said, "I had seen bruises where Tom had thrown his mom up against the wall in an argument. . . . They were just arguing and he just grabbed ahold of her and threw her" (*People v. Odle*, 1986).

Excerpt from Yvonne Sexton's Testimony

ALLING: What was the general information that Carolyn would give you on how Tom treated the other children?

SEXTON: Well, you know, sometimes he'd twist their arms or hit them, you know.
ALLING: Did she indicate to you that she was frightened of Tom?
SEXTON: Yes, she did.
ALLING: Did she indicate that the children were frightened of Tom?
SEXTON: Yes.

During cross-examination, defense attorney Henson tried to get Sexton to open up about Carolyn's parenting skills. Sexton acknowledged that Carolyn had had significant difficulty dealing with her children, in general, and frequently placed responsibility for the care and safety of her three younger children in Tom's hands, requiring that he babysit the other children on an almost daily basis while she pursued her social obligations and recreational activities, such as bowling.

During the prosecution's redirect, Sexton testified that she was aware that Sean had also been involved in antisocial activities as well, but she was unaware of such activities with regard to Robyn or Scott (*People v. Odle*, 1986).

A former neighbor, Alan Hale, who testified next, said that Tom "terrorized the entire neighborhood through acts of vandalism. . . . It seemed to develop and escalate. The longer we lived there, the worse it got. . . . We moved because I refused to be intimidated." Hale talked about gardens being trampled, Peeping Tom incidents, and rocks thrown at people and passing cars—including his. He also testified that he witnessed Tom committing acts of violence on his brothers and instigating them to commit acts of vandalism and mischief. When he confronted the boy, Tom adamantly denied the accusations, but Hale didn't believe him: "I didn't observe truthfulness. I felt as though he had mastered the ability to lie to anyone about anything." He also testified that Carolyn would deny such accusations against her son and refuse to consider the possibility that her son was harassing Hale and his family (*People v. Odle*, 1986).

Hale said he contacted Robert Odle about the behavior, which, "[s]eemed to stall the situation, temporarily. . . . but then it started up again. There were a couple of occasions where we had broken glass or bottles thrown on our porch. The back windshield of my wife's car was shot out by a pellet rifle. The driver's side door of my pick-up truck was shot out. The radiator—holes were shot in the radiator of the truck by a pellet rifle." Hale connected all the incidents to Tom Odle.

Under cross-examination, attorney Henson asked Hale to clarify his "Peeping Tom" statement.

Excerpt from Alan Hale's Testimony

HENSON: You said that there was an incident of some Peeping Tom type incidents. Did you ever see Tom doing something of that nature?

HALE: Outside my bedroom window with my own eyes, I sure did.

HENSON: When was that?

HALE: It was within a year prior to our moving.

HENSON: And was that day or night?

HALE: That was after dusk.

Hale went on to say that he called the police, but they did not arrest Tom. Hale spoke to Robert about the incident and told him "if something wasn't done soon, I was going to press charges." He related another incident that happened after they moved away from the neighborhood, in which Tom stood in the middle of the street and wouldn't let Mrs. Hale drive her car into the Hales' driveway.

Mr. Hale called the police on Tom on more than one occasion. He felt that Tom retaliated by calling the police on Hale every chance he got: "The calls that I made to the police were a tenth of the calls the Odles made to the police for us. The police were aware that there was a problem in the neighborhood." But no one was ever arrested (*People v. Odle*, 1986).

Maurice Yeargin was at one time the Odle's next-door neighbor. He testified that when Tom was a young child, Yeargin and Tom were "buddies. I took him to the ballgame over at St. Louis with me and we found—we took him with us." He reported that Tom's character began to change when he was about fourteen years old: "I lived next door to him from I guess the time he was born. I moved away from him three and a half years ago. He drove me away. . . . I told his dad, I said, I have lived here over 37 years and a 16-year-old kid run me off and he had—I couldn't get the police to do anything." The prosecution wanted to know what Tom did to drive them away: "[H]e was so mean to my daughter and that was the main thing and he was always making obscene gestures at my wife and her both. . . . my wife—my daughter couldn't get out of the house. She was just a prisoner in her house."

Yeargin related an incident where Tom entered Yeargin's house without permission. He said that on a typical Friday evening, his family would leave the house to go to supper, and Tom would watch them from the picture window, making obscene gestures at them as they left. On one occasion, the Yeargins returned home early, "and the back window had been broken out of the dining room." They found a muddy footprint on the garage floor and were sure the police could find fingerprints on the window. The police checked out the incident but said the conditions weren't good for checking either fingerprints or footprints.

At the time, the Yeargins thought nothing had been stolen. But later in the week, when his wife went to get her tithe money for church, she discovered it was missing. Again, the police were called, and no investigation ensued.

Yeargin also described a number of incidents where Tom had been physically cruel to his brothers. Henson asked about that during cross-examination.

Excerpt from Maurice Yeargin's Testimony

YEARGIN: He was always mean to Sean ever since I knew him.

HENSON: Was anybody else in that family mean to Sean?

YEARGIN: All of them.

HENSON: All of them were mean to Sean?

YEARGIN: Yes. She [Carolyn] told my wife that when she was carrying Sean, she hated him and she hated him from then on. After he was born, she hated him. She encouraged all the kids to hate him. None of the kids liked him. (*People v. Odle*, 1986)

Tom Bolerjack and Gene Bolerjack owned a neighborhood grocery store, Bolerjack's Market, through December 1985. Tom Bolerjack testified that Tom Odle had tried to cash a two-party check written off his grandmother's account. Bolerjack was suspicious because of his previous dealings with Odle and called the grandmother, who instructed him not to cash the check because she had not written it.

Tom Bolerjack's suspicions stemmed from Tom's frequent attempts at shoplifting from the store. Both Tom and Gene testified that Sean had been caught shoplifting as well. Sean told them that Tom "made him" shoplift. Both Bolerjacks agreed that after conversations with Robert Odle, the shoplifting would stop for a while but would always resume (*People v. Odle*, 1986).

Seventeen-year-old Rebecca Hanson testified that she "used to go out with him [Tom Odle] about three and a half years ago." At that time, she was thirteen, and Tom was sixteen. They dated for less than a month. Alling asked, "Did Tom ever make you sneak out of your home?" Rebecca said, "I did, yeah."

Excerpt from Rebecca Hanson's Testimony

ALLING: Can you describe what that was? Why you did that?

HANSON: Yeah. He used to call me and he used to say—asked me if I wanted to go out and I'd say no, I can't go or something and then he'd say, well, if you don't, I'm going to have to see what happens to you or my mom and dad.

ALLING: Did you take that as a threat against you and your family?

HANSON: That's the way I took it.   (*People v. Odle*, 1986)

In order to substantiate the claims made about Tom's character, Crego asked to read details of previous proceedings against Tom Odle in 1983, and the court agreed. He read transcripts from Tom's testimony during an investigation that alleged he had sex with a minor. In graphic detail, Tom described the sexual act with the girl who was in sixth grade at the time. Alling also read juvenile criminal charges against Tom Odle: "[H]e was adjudicated as delinquent for one count of felony theft, four counts of residential burglary, four counts of misdemeanor theft and one count of attempt residential burglary."

She concluded, "We're asking that the court consider these as part of the evidence offered here at sentencing hearing in aggravation of the offenses that the Defendant's been found guilty of." After some unsuccessful wrangling by the defense team, the proceedings were entered into evidence (*People v. Odle*, 1986).

Richard Williams and George Buretz were law-enforcement officers who worked at the Jefferson County Jail. They both testified that Tom was a model prisoner. Williams, who gave drug-prevention talks in the county, also said, "I was asking him about his drug use and he made the comment that he wished he could help people get off drugs and that started me thinking about maybe making a videotape." Tom said that he would like to make such a tape (*People vs. Odle*, 1986).

The defense called Dicky Dennis, a friend of Tom Odle, who recalled seeing Tom at high school one day and overheard Tom tell another person "that he had another disagreement with his father. . . . It looked like somebody had just hauled off and decked him in the face" (*People v. Odle*, 1986).

The defense's final witness was Evelyn Eller, Carolyn Odle's mother and Tom's grandmother.

Excerpt from Evelyn Eller's Testimony

HENSON: Do you have an opinion as to whether or not Tom Odle should receive the death penalty?

ELLER: I'm not for the death penalty, no.   (*People v. Odle*, 1986)

Sentencing Arguments

Following Eller's single statement to the court, the sentencing arguments began. Prosecutor Alling led with the state's argument for the death penalty: "The task for the death penalty is the most serious recommendation any prosecutor can ever make. From the first day these brutal murders were discovered, it was obvious that the death penalty was an appropriate sentence under the laws of Illinois. But as responsible prosecutors, we felt that as much information that was available about Tom Odle and his victims should be uncovered and considered before any final decision could be made. It was not until the lengthy trial of this Defendant had ended that the decision to seek the death penalty was made by my office.

"Several factors were especially important in making this determination. The premeditation, the number of victims involved, the relationship of the victims to their murderer, the age of the children that were killed, the brutality inflicted upon the members of the family and Defendant's total lack of remorse at terminating their lives.

"Defendant's history reveals him as a bully who terrorized a neighborhood, an accomplished liar who preyed on the elderly and the young. He was an individual who engaged in sexual acts with minors. He illegally possessed and sold drugs. He committed residential burglaries, shopliftings, thefts, forgery, batteries, sale of stolen goods and intimidations. And then when he was too well known in this community to steal himself, he forced his eight-year-old brother to enter a life of crime and do his stealing for him.

"Tom Odle is not a one-time criminal. His documented lack of self-respect for people and property date back to at least 1981. The vicious murders of his family is foreign to the way of life in any society, not just ours, but our law states that the punishment should fit the crime. We respect the law and we believe that it dictates that Tom Odle should receive the death penalty. . . . We respectfully request that Tom Odle be sentenced to death" (*People v. Odle*, 1986).

Defense attorney Henson argued that the "State's Attorney doesn't understand the importance of the evidence we have presented at this trial. . . . This case is about a family situation that is very unique which probably will not be seen in years to come. Has not been seen in past years. And I think that our evidence at the trial bore that out."

He next cited case law, *Godfrey v. Georgia*, 1980, *Eddings v. Oklahoma*, 1982, and *Illinois v. Carrus Buggs*, 1986, and proposed that these were similar cases in terms of the nature of the crimes. In each case, the prosecution sought the death penalty because of the suffering of the victims. In each case, the death penalty was denied because the courts felt there were more egregious circumstances—torture and severe abuse—for which the death penalty should be saved. He further argued that Dr. Garretson stated the deaths were almost instantaneous and, so, similar to those stated in the referenced cases.

Henson reiterated the mitigating circumstances of the Tom Odle case: the unusually dysfunctional family dynamic that led to severe emotional problems, the restricted activities in the formative years, the documented history of physical and mental abuse, the failure of DCFS to correct the family's problems or recognize the extent of them, the drug and alcohol abuse, Tom's personality disorder, and the ultimate act of abuse—being kicked out of the family home. Time and again, Henson brought up the consequences of being raised by a sadistic mother and a passive father: "Now, I just don't feel . . . that a person that is in that state of mind should receive the death penalty. That's not what the death penalty is there for" (*People v. Odle*, 1986).

Alling promptly restated her case: "His family life did not give him a license to kill. That message should be stated loud and clear by this court. The mitigating factors of his family life are not sufficient to preclude the imposition of the death sentence" (*People v. Odle*, 1986).

Before sentencing, Judge Garrison allowed Tom Odle to address the court: "Your Honor, in response to the State's accusation that I have no remorse, they're dead wrong. I may not be like a normal individual when it comes to feelings, remorse and general stuff like that. I look at it as this way: I'm sorry for what I did and I feel that I should be punished, but—but sitting around crying, walking around like a zombie is not going to bring them back. I would like to remember them the way they was, the good times, the bad times. That's all I have left.

"They might not have been the best parents in the world, but in some terms, they were good parents. I can just say that I'm going to cherish all the good times and the bad times we all shared together" (*People v. Odle*, 1986).

At 9:00 A.M. the following day, Tom Odle was sentenced to death for the murders of Robert, Carolyn, Sean, Robyn, and Scott Odle. Tom was going to death row for eventual execution.

> When I was given the death penalty I had no real feeling, which was probably why the judge said I lacked remorse. I knew I was in deep trouble during the penalty phase of the whole thing. They found me death eligible and I knew it was over. I was sent back to the prosecuting county for sentencing because my lawyers thought the judge there would not send me to death row. But he did.

10

Life on Death Row

At the age of nineteen, Tom Odle was the youngest death-row inmate in the Illinois prison system. He spent the next ten years in the condemned unit at the Menard Correctional Center, one of the oldest prisons in Illinois. Built in 1878, Menard is a daunting structure cut from the sandstone on the bank of the Mississippi River about sixty miles south of East Saint Louis.

Like all other death-row inmates, he was confined to his cell twenty-two and a half hours per day. His death-row cell at Menard was nine feet wide by nine feet long by nine and a half feet high. The gray, concrete cell walls, floor, and ceiling were cold and scarred by rust stains that had bled through the paint. A stainless-steel toilet and sink were bolted to the wall opposite the bars. A six-feet-by-three-feet cot was bolted to the floor and wall. For one and a half hours per day, he was allowed to exercise outside of his cell and socialize in the prison yard with other death-row inmates, the likes of which included hard-core psychopaths, such as John Wayne Gacy, who was convicted of the murders of thirty-three teenage boys and young men. Aside from Gacy, whom he despised, Tom developed friendships with other condemned-unit inmates and lifers. In fact, the older inmates taught him how to survive in prison and protected him from the violent psychopaths and sexual predators.

> Walking through the doors of Illinois Death Row at the age
> of 19, the youngest at the time to have received the ultimate
> punishment, I was scared to death. I was scared to death:
> 140 pounds, I had no hair on my face, I had long hair, I tried

to inflate myself to make myself look bigger, hold in as much air as my lungs and chest will hold, and not look so scared. You know you hear all of the stories about a pretty white boy going to the joint. He's gonna be chosen as somebody's wife and all that stuff. I heard my share of them. I was trying to make myself look bigger. I was scared to death.

Once I got there though, the stories proved to be wrong. The image that the public has of these guys, that they are foaming at the mouth, the worst of the worst, proved to be false, for the most part. Don't get me wrong. There were some really bizarre characters, like John Wayne Gacy. But for the most part, as a whole, we took care of each other. It was like a big family. Everybody took me in because I was the youngest; took me in, tried to educate me. "You need to do this, don't do that." Then they explained the appeals process and what I needed to do to help with my appeals. I mean they gave me some good pointers. I didn't need to walk around with my chest inflated. Bobby Lewis, Tony Guest, Daryl Simms and William Bracy, most of them really helped me.

My expectations of Death Row and the reality of Death Row were as different as night and day. In the movies you see young white kids coming to prison and becoming prey to the predators time and time again, but that was far from what actually took place. The old saying "it takes a village to raise a child" came into play. Most of the men there were in their thirties and forties and they embraced me like a son as they told me what would happen on Death Row and in the courts during the appeals process. They were always willing to answer any questions I had about anything and strongly encouraged me to get involved in my appeals because nobody knew my case better than I did.

The Death-Row Population

According to Death Penalty Information Center (DPIC) (2011), from 1976 to 2011, there were 1,277 executions in the United States. The year that Tom Odle stepped onto death row 1986, there were 18 executions. The peak year during that time period was 1999 with 98.

Of those executed from 1976 to 2011, 716 were white, 441 were African American, 96 were Hispanic, and 24 were classified as "Other" with respect to race. The race ratio of death-row inmates varies from those executed: 44 percent were white, 42 percent African American, 12 percent Hispanic, and 2 percent "Other." There were 61 women on death row as of December 31, 2012, representing 1.93 percent of the death-row population. Twelve women have been executed since 1976.

With respect to the societal effects of the death penalty, 88 percent of polled academic criminologists, including many of the former and current presidents of the American Society of Criminology, reject the notion that the death penalty acts as a deterrent to murder (Radelet & Lacock, 2009). According to the Illinois Coalition to Abolish the Death Penalty (ICADP) (2011), death-penalty cases, from trial to execution, cost states eight to ten times more than the cost of life without parole. And, according to the DPIC (2011), every state that has done a cost study has found that death-penalty cases cost millions more than non-death cases, including cases that receive life without parole.

Furthermore, the strongest argument against the death penalty in contemporary society is the ominous risk of execution of the innocent following wrongful convictions. According to the DPIC (2011), 139 death-row inmates have been exonerated and released from prison during the past four decades in the United States. Nearly half of these exonerations occurred in four states: Illinois, Florida, Texas, and Oklahoma; over 30 percent of all exonerations occurred in Illinois and Florida. Although the principle of retributive justice as expressed in the "eye for an eye" philosophy is appealing to many, particularly given its biblical origins, the American justice system is far from flawless. As such, the possibility that an individual may be executed for crimes that he or she did not commit is a disturbing reality of the death penalty.

> I spent my time playing basketball, lifting weights, playing cards and dominos or just watching television. I wrote a lot of letters to my friends. I also responded to letters from girls who managed to find my address and wrote to tell me how cool they thought I was because I had murdered my parents. That was one thing I ate up at that time because it diminished my responsibility and guilt. It was remarkable that so many teenagers, especially sexually abused girls, praised my courage and strength with regard to the manner in which I had retaliated against my abusers. At the time, it made me feel like I had done a great service to mankind by committing this horrific act of violence which, of course, I used to justify my actions and repress my guilt.

Now, after many years of growth and self-examination, I often wonder what happened to those troubled teens who praised me. It disturbs me more now knowing that the horrible crime for which I am singularly responsible and which ended the lives of my parents and siblings and shattered my community could have taken place in so many other homes with a large wake of ripples flowing through families like a hot knife through butter.

My routine was very simple in the beginning: staying up all night, going to the yard, rain, sleet or shine, watching T.V. or listening to the radio. My time seemed to be going by uneventfully until I allowed a reporter from a local newspaper, the Southern Illinoisan, to interview me on a visit. My objective was to demonstrate that I was not a vicious animal or some evil creature, as I had been portrayed in the media. Unfortunately, it didn't turn out the way I had hoped. I was extremely naïve with respect to reporters and the media, in general. As a result, I was portrayed as a remorseless, cold-blooded killer, devoid of normal emotions. I learned a hard lesson in trust.

About that time, I had my first altercation with the correctional staff in response to an institutional policy that I believe was employed to humiliate and dehumanize Death Row inmates. The policy requires that, following a visit, the inmate must bend over and pull his buttocks apart so they can see his anus. Obviously, this is very degrading and they knew it and still know it. But when they started employing the procedure, the guards would walk down the gallery laughing and taunting the individuals who were forced to submit themselves to this abusive act. As a result, I made up my mind I would not comply.

So, after my next visit I knew what was going to happen. After the visit they shake you down to ensure you aren't bringing any contraband back into the facility. The shakedown is a strip search that includes the aforementioned spreading of your butt cheeks so they can examine your anus. So, after I stripped naked, they told me to bend over and spread my cheeks. But I didn't do it. I did not say a word. I just stood there naked and after a short while I started getting dressed. So, they decided it was time to teach me a lesson. Five or six members of the correctional staff jumped on me, knocked me around and beat me. Then, they handcuffed me and beat me some more. But I did not bend over and spread my cheeks, because I was not going to be degraded and humiliated, just because some loved ones had visited me.

I ended up going to segregation for that incident, which consisted of confinement to my cell 24 hours per day for an extended period of time. But I gained the respect of my peers at the same time. After that incident, I started lifting weights on a regular basis, because at that time I weighed only about 150 pounds and wasn't very muscular. I knew that the next time it wouldn't be so easy for them to knock me around and I would easily absorb the hits and kicks if I had a little more weight.

While in segregation, one guy in particular respected me for taking a stand against the policy on anal examinations and helped me to start weight training. He also taught me how to box and physically defend myself in anticipation of the possibility that I should ever find myself in that situation again. From then on, I lifted weights with fierceness because never again was I going to be anyone's whipping boy.

Things were pretty uneventful from then on. I went back to my daily routine until they found some weed in my cell and back to seg I went. Later, I came out of seg, but went back in shortly thereafter for getting drunk on some prison hooch. Prison hooch is really nasty stuff, but once you're getting buzzed, the taste doesn't really matter. You just chase that buzz. While drunk on hooch, I cussed a few people out, passed out, and went back to seg for quite a while.

But, it's important to understand that there was nothing cool or noble about my behavior or situation at that time. I was on Death Row to be executed for the murders of my family. I was a kid trying to deal with the courts and lawyers whom I began to believe did not have my best interests at heart. I've lived with the haunting images of what led me to Death Row, plagued with a sense of hopelessness as other people continued on with their lives while I remained in a purgatory where time stands still. I used drugs in prison the same way I used them in the world, to numb my pain and the guilt I was toting around like a ball and chain. I blamed everyone but myself for my problems. At that time, I even believed my guilt was someone else's fault. And that useless cycle of self-deception continued day after day, year after year. There is no glory on Death Row. It isn't a rec center or holiday get-a-way. It is your own personal hell that you are going to have to eventually confront before the time will start to move—otherwise, you are basically a shell of a human being.

Legal Representation

According to an article by two *Chicago Tribune* investigative reporters, thirty-three of those defendants sentenced to death in Illinois from 1977 to 1999 had been represented by "an attorney who had been, or was later, disbarred or suspended—disciplinary sanctions reserved for conduct so incompetent, unethical or even criminal that the state believes an attorney's license should be taken away." And twenty-six death-row inmates "have received a new trial or sentencing because their attorneys' incompetence rendered the verdict or sentence unfair, court records show" (Armstrong & Mills, 1999).

> After about two years on Death Row, my appeal was denied and another execution date was set. Two more attorneys were assigned to continue the appeal process, which happened without one even knowing about it, so I had to fire them from my case. Eventually, my case became one of attorney Richard Cunningham's many death penalty cases. My taste for lawyers up until that point had become very sour. After my conviction, I had an attorney that I felt blew me off on appeals to the Illinois Supreme Court. Then, I had two more attorneys that really did nothing at all. I thought this was happening because I was young and really didn't know any better. After all, these were lawyers who were supposed to ethically have my best interest at heart.
>
> I became very active in my case after that. I decided I was not going to be executed just because I passively stayed stupid and let someone else control my destiny. After my initial conversation with Mr. Cunningham I liked him. He was down to earth, with no high expectations. He kept it straight and simple and I respected him. Over the years that he was my attorney, we developed a friendship.

On a personal note, I have come to realize through the years, that most women who get involved with men on Death Row are damaged in some way. That isn't necessarily a bad thing. There are some very righteous women out there who have the humanistic view that all people are good. However, they sometimes make very bad decisions. I have been blessed in knowing a few of these women and they have done their best to help me conquer my guilt and hopelessness. They all helped me in some way and I will forever be grateful to them. A couple of them showed me the meaning of unconditional love, but due to the visitation restrictions of Death Row and miscommunication because of lost mail, late mail or un-placed phone calls due to confinement in seg or lockdowns, those relationships faded away.

It takes a hell of a strong woman to walk in these shoes with me. A couple managed to do it for a little while and they truly brightened up some gloomy days. I'll never forget the gifts they gave me. For those gifts of unconditional love, friendship, and partnership, I will forever be grateful.

I met [name withheld] and we ended up getting married a few months later. It was all good at the beginning, but then the bricks began falling away and I could see the structure underneath, which was really damaged; in fact, damaged more than me, so it didn't last but a short while.

Back in the News

After nearly nine years on death row and not long after he divorced his wife, Tom Odle granted another interview. This time he spoke to Randy Snyder, Mt. Vernon bureau chief for the *Morning Sentinel.* These are excerpts from that story.

He won't be 29 until December 20. Yet he has spent a third of his life in the condemned unit—Death Row—on a bluff overlooking the Mississippi River, a picturesque sight as one faces west but considerably less so when one turns to view the grim façade of the Maximum Security Unit of this aging facility. . . . Odle got his first look at Death Row on July 3, 1986.

"What went through my mind?" Odle repeated the question during an exclusive interview on Thursday at a visiting room not far from his cell. "I was a 130-pound, 18-year-old white boy coming to Death Row. What do you think was going through my mind? I was scared as hell."

At the time, Odle was the youngest person in Illinois ever to be placed in a condemned unit. . . . "I want to tell my side of the story, even though I know it's going to cause my family, especially my [maternal] grandmother, a lot of pain to have all this brought up again."

At the time, Tom's case was up for appeals.

Odle's appeal is being based on contention that his court-appointed counsel at the trial-court level was inadequate and that [Tom] was under the influence of hard drugs 10 years ago.

"The average murder appeals process runs 15 to 17 years," Odle said, "so I figure I've got maybe seven or eight more years left to try and get out of here."

His 9½ years at Menard have not been uneventful. He has gotten married, but now says he seeks a divorce and has a new girlfriend. Odle says he has also converted to Catholicism, has kicked the cigarette habit and no longer drinks "hooch," a prison underground alcohol drink made from just about anything that ferments. The shoulder-length hair he displays in his prison identification photo is gone. . . . [H]is hair was similar to a style he wore a decade ago.

Odle contends the changes are more than physical. "The Tommy Odle who did those things 10 years ago is dead," he said. "Tom Odle today would not think of doing such things; he knows there are other ways to deal with problems.

"If Tom Odle got out of here tomorrow, he would be John Q. Citizen with a 9-to-5 job, a beautiful wife, beautiful kids, station wagon, home every night. Those are the things I want out of what's left of my life."

Odle says he stopped smoking cigarettes about 1½ years ago. "I decided that if I can beat this [indicating his surroundings] I'll be damned if I'm going to let cancer get me.

"One Christmas a few years ago I had to go to the hospital after drinking a bunch of hooch. I had a blood-alcohol level of something like 0.24. That cured me of drinking."

Odle says he regrets getting the tattoos that adorn most of both arms.

"I did most of them myself right after I got in here. It's done with underground materials. What can they do once they're on there? Back then, I had to show everybody I was tough, you know. I wouldn't do it now."

He says another inmate's influence led to his conversion to Catholicism about 2½ years ago. "I was a Protestant but this guy got me interested in being a Catholic, so I studied it for a long time and decided it was more in line with what I believe."

Odle says his current existence finds him locked in a private cell 21 hours Mondays through Saturdays and all day Sunday unless he has visitors. "I get an hour and a half a day to use the law library and another hour and a half a day in the yard."

Odle says he uses the yard time to lift weights or play basketball, a skill he acquired only after going to prison. "Hey, I was a druggie before," he says.

The exercise has obviously paid dividends; Odle's t-shirt could not hide considerable upper body development. "I'm not a skinny little kid anymore.

"I usually go to bed about 8 P.M. and wake up at 3:30 or 4:00 A.M. because that's about the only time it gets quiet around here," he said. "Then I can read or just think.

"My TV is my 'cellie' [roommate]; it's usually on, but I'm not always watching it. We get basic cable TV and an institutional channel that shows recently released movies. It's paid for by the Inmate Trust Fund, which gets money from a percentage of the vending machines and so on."

He added: "I've got a pet. It's a little, bitty field mouse about the size of my thumb. I made him a house by melting some food cartons together."

Odle says his current neighbors are respectful of one another. "Nobody is trying to drown each other out by turning up the volume on their TVs or stereos. I use my headphones if I want my TV loud."

Tom told Snyder how difficult it was watching friends disappear.

"One thing that's tough is making friends in here and then watching them being taken out [to Stateville Correctional Center in Joliet for execution] and knowing they won't be back."

Odle . . . said that if he had to do it over, he would have kept his job and apartment in Covington, KY, a Cincinnati suburb where he lived before returning to Mount Vernon in the fall of 1985.

"I had a little place, nothing fancy, but it was mine, and a beat-up old van," he said. "I didn't have much money for drugs and alcohol because it took most of what I earned to keep a roof over my head."

"They [parents] wanted me to come home, so I did. A son of a friend of theirs had killed himself playing Russian roulette, and they said they were afraid I might do something like that. Then they told me I couldn't live there anymore," Odle said. "In fact, I had played Russian roulette several times, usually by myself in my room [at home] with this .22 pistol I had."

Reflecting on the day of the murders, Tom told Snyder that he was going to take Theresa home the morning after the murders and then commit suicide by driving the family car into something so that he would die in the collision. Additionally, although no one witnessed him playing Russian roulette, such behavior was consistent with the suicidal ideation that he reportedly manifested, intermittently, prior to the murders.

Twenty-five years after the murders, Tom recalled his experiences playing Russian roulette:

> As far as Russian roulette, I had played a few times. I'm not quite sure how many times, more than a couple and not more than five. I was using a .22 revolver that was my father's and it was loaded with only one bullet. I would get home late at night, around 11–12. Everyone would be asleep. I would smoke a joint or two, listen to music, and play solitaire until I would get tired enough to go to bed. Before I would go to sleep, I would get my father's .22 revolver, go back to my room, and unload it. I would put one bullet in, spin the chamber, lock it, put it in my mouth, and pull the trigger. I was tired of not knowing who I was, where I was going, and not being able to answer the question of what was wrong with me. One morning I got up and nobody was home, except Dad, who was leaving to run some errands. I decided to play then and something inside me said 'point it at the ceiling,' which I did and pulled the trigger. It went off, scaring the hell out of me. I told Dad it was an accident, but I don't think he believed me. He took the gun and hid it. I never played again after that. I guess that woke me up from that idea of doing something to myself.

During the Snyder interview, Tom expressed his views regarding his trial attorneys and the formation of a Tom Odle Fan Club.

He also contends his court-appointed attorneys, James Henson and Charl Stowe, were incompetent. Henson is still Jefferson County public defender. Stowe was fired as an assistant defender by the County Board shortly after the Odle trial after it was revealed Stowe had run up a telephone bill of several hundred dollars calling from his Olney motel to his father's law firm in Greenville.

Formation of a Tommy Odle Fan Club made the Associated Press wire at the time as teens who saw themselves in similar situations made Odle a cult hero of sorts.

"I got letters from kids saying they'd thought about killing their parents," Odle said. "My girlfriend has told me that she felt like that before. I guess a lot of kids consider it. But the difference is, they didn't cross that line. But a fan club named after me? That's sick."

Toward the end of the interview, Tom became introspective.

"I don't accept my situation," he said, his blue eyes hardening. "I deal with it."

And he notes: "You'd be surprised what you miss in here. I miss seeing the stars. From my cell I can see absolutely beautiful sunsets on the river. But the angle of my window is such that I can't see the stars. I also miss certain smells, but mostly, I miss the smell of freedom.

"Be sure and put this in your article: Maybe you could end with it. Just tell any kids out there that no matter how bad things may seem at the time, there's always a way out if you'll just stop and think, use your head. And stay away from the damned drugs. Tell them to write to me and I'll write them back. I wish I had someone to talk to."

While Tom waited for the appeals process to take its course, the battle over the death penalty nationally and in Illinois, in particular, continued to be waged.

Less than four years after Tom was sentenced to death, the State of Illinois carried out its first execution, based on the death-penalty statute established in 1977. On September 12, 1990, Charles Walker, who had been convicted of the double murder of a couple in East Saint Louis and sentenced to death, was executed by lethal injection at the Stateville Correctional Center in Joliet, Illinois (Center on Wrongful Convictions, 2011).

> The strangest time for me was when the state of Illinois started executing people again in 1990. All of a sudden, individuals who had been my neighbors for years were being led away to be murdered by the State. I knew their families, had broken bread with them, and had enjoyed yard with them.

One neighbor, George Delvecchio, had a heart attack one week before his scheduled date with the needle. They rushed him out to the hospital, treated him, and returned him in time for his execution. That blew my mind.

When John Wayne Gacy was executed, the prison staff rushed to clean out his cell so they could claim his sheets and rug and anything else left behind. I was amazed. Why would anyone want to touch, let alone possess that man's sheets? Even more bizarre behavior came from some of the inmates on Death Row who you would think would feel some sort of empathy. They would start sending notes to the soon-to-be executed person asking him for some of his property. It was disgusting. A few people left me some of their things when they left, but I couldn't keep them. I just pushed them under my bed until I could eventually send the stuff to their families. As a whole, we were like a big family comprised of diverse personalities that would pull together in times of need or even revolt against the staff. But there were times that really made me wonder, what is this guy's deal?

Wrongful Convictions and the Road to the Moratorium

Many men that Tom Odle knew and spent time with on death row ultimately left the row for a final trip to Joliet. Others met different fates, as the sticky brew of the Illinois death penalty continued to boil, and new evidence rose through the mire to the surface for all to see.

In 1994, John Wayne Gacy was eventually executed after the lethal-injection apparatus malfunctioned on the first attempt. Four months after Gacy was executed, Joseph Burrows, who had been convicted of the murder of a farmer in Iroquois County in 1988 and sentenced to death, was exonerated based on evidence that Gayle Potter, the woman who actually committed the murder, had falsely implicated Burrows and another man in the crime (Center on Wrongful Convictions, 2011).

In March 1995, the State of Illinois executed two men on the same day in the first double execution in forty years. James Free and Hernando Williams died within an hour of each other at the hands of a contract executioner at the Stateville Correctional Center in Joliet. Two months later, Girvies Davis was executed for a murder in Saint Clair County following the denial of clemency by Governor James Edgar, despite evidence investigative journalism students at Northwestern University produced that casts serious doubt with respect to his guilt. And, in September 1995, Charles Albanese was executed for the murder of three of his relatives (Center on Wrongful Convictions, 2011).

In November 1995, Rolando Cruz was acquitted for the kidnapping, rape, and murder of ten-year-old Jeanine Nicarico. Cruz and Alejandro Hernandez were wrongfully convicted of the crimes in 1985 in DuPage County as a result of the perjured testimony of police officers who lied that Cruz had provided them with information about the crime that implicated him as the killer. Despite the fact that the lead detective in the case resigned in protest insisting that the state's attorney was prosecuting the wrong men, Cruz and Hernandez were prosecuted, convicted, and sentenced to death. Following their conviction, a serial rapist and murderer named Brian Dugan confessed to the crime. Nevertheless, the prosecutors refused to acknowledge their wrongful conviction of Cruz and Hernandez. In 1994, during his third trial in which DNA evidence was presented that conclusively confirmed that Dugan had raped the girl, one of the police officers admitted that he had lied during his previous testimony about Cruz's statements to the police. As a result of such compelling evidence, Cruz was acquitted. One month later, Hernandez was also exonerated (Center on Wrongful Convictions, 2011). Two weeks before Hernandez was exonerated, George DelVecchio was executed for the 1977 murder of six-year-old Tony Canzoneri during the robbery of the boy's home.

During a seven-month period from June to December 1996, four more men were exonerated and freed from death row in Illinois. Two of these men, Verneal Jimerson and Dennis Williams, were convicted of a double murder in 1978, which the media labeled the Ford Heights Four case. Based on evidence that included witness coercion, perjury, false testimony, and prosecutorial misconduct, Jimerson and Williams were exonerated in the summer of 1996 (Center on Wrongful Convictions, 2011). Two months later, Raymond Lee Stewart was executed for murdering six people in a killing spree in Rockford, Illinois, in 1981, to which he had repeatedly confessed.

In October 1996, Gary Gauger was exonerated for the 1993 murder of his parents when the Illinois Appellate Court ruled that the police in rural McHenry County lacked probable cause to arrest him for the murders. During his original trial, no physical evidence was presented to implicate Gauger. However, the McHenry County sheriff's deputies who interrogated him testified that he had confessed, despite the fact that no electronic or written record of his confession could be produced. Based on the deputies' questionable testimony and that of a repeated felon recruited by the prosecution who was in the same jail while Gauger awaited trial, Gauger was convicted of the double murder and sentenced to death. Less than a year following Gauger's exoneration, two members of the Wisconsin Outlaws, a motorcycle gang, were indicted for the murders. They were later convicted of the crimes (Center on Wrongful Convictions, 2011).

In December 1996, Carl Lawson, convicted of the murder of eight-year-old Terrence Jones in East Saint Louis in 1989 and sentenced to death, was acquitted during his second postconviction retrial. Lawson, who was a friend of the boy's mother, had been convicted based solely on evidence that his shoe print was found at the scene of the crime. Although Lawson testified that his shoe print was present because he was called to the boy's home after his body was found, the prosecution dramatically claimed that the shoe print, which was partially made in blood, must have been the killer's. Lawson was the ninth exonerated death-row inmate in nine years (Center on Wrongful Convictions, 2011).

On November 22, 1997, the second double execution in two years was carried out at the Stateville Correctional Center. Walter Stewart, convicted of the 1980 murder of jewelry-store owner Thomas Pavlopoulos and store employee Danilo Rodica, and Durlyn Eddmonds, convicted of the rape and murder of nine-year-old Richard Miller in 1977, were executed within two hours of each other. Stewart and Eddmonds marked the ninth and tenth executions, respectively, since the reinstatement of the death penalty in 1977. In January 1998 was the eleventh execution since 1977. In 1990, Lloyd Wayne Hampton robbed and murdered sixty-nine-year-old Roy Pendleton in a motel room in Madison County. Prior to his execution, he stated that he accepted responsibility for his crime and made no excuses. Hampton declined the customary last meal and simply requested a Coke and cigarettes.

Later that year, Anthony Porter was granted a reprieve by the Illinois Supreme Court fifty hours prior to his scheduled execution because a psychological evaluation revealed that Porter's IQ was in the moderately mentally retarded range. He had been convicted of the 1982 murders of Marilyn Green and Jerry Hillard on the south side of Chicago. At that time, it was still legal to execute the mentally retarded in Illinois. However, his intellectual status drew into question his competency to be executed. The reprieve allowed a team of volunteer attorneys, investigators, and the group of Northwestern University journalism students to investigate the case. The investigation revealed that Porter had been wrongfully convicted and provided evidence that a man named Alstory Simon had killed Green and Hillard. In February 1999, Porter became the tenth death-row inmate to be exonerated. Two weeks later, Steven Smith became the eleventh death-row prisoner to be exonerated when the Illinois Supreme Court reversed his conviction. The court held as unreliable the "eye witness" testimony of a prosecution witness and crack addict named Debrah Caraway, whose testimony was singularly responsible for convicting him of the murder of Virdeen Willis in a Chicago South Side bar in 1985 (Center on Wrongful Convictions, 2011).

Shortly following the exonerations of Porter and Smith in February 1999, Andrew Kokoraleis was executed at the Tamms Correctional Center in Southern Illinois. He had been sentenced to death for the abduction and murder of twenty-one-year-old Lorraine Borowski in 1982 and had received a life sentence for the murder of Rose Beck Davis. Governor George Ryan denied Kokoraleis clemency but agonized over his decision to deny clemency that arose so closely on the heels of Porter's and Smith's exonerations one month before. In a formal statement, Ryan announced, "I must admit that it is very difficult to hold in your hands the life of any person, even a person who, in the eyes of the many, has acted so horrendously as to have forfeited any right to any consideration of mercy. I have struggled with this issue of the death penalty and still feel that some crimes are so horrendous and so heinous that society has a right to demand the ultimate penalty" (Center on Wrongful Convictions, 2011).

Two months after Kokoraleis's execution, the twelfth execution in ten years, Ronald Jones became the twelfth death-row inmate to be exonerated in a period of twelve years. Despite the lack of any physical evidence linking Jones to the murder, a Cook County circuit-court judge convicted and sentenced Jones to death for the 1985 rape and murder of a young woman on Chicago's South Side. Jones had testified that his signed confession was the result of relentless beatings by Chicago police detectives. His attorney, Richard "Dick" Cunningham (also Odle's lawyer), legendary death-row lawyer and former assistant Illinois appellate defender, obtained DNA testing that conclusively revealed that the semen recovered from the victim did not come from Jones. As a result, the prosecutors eventually dropped the charges against Jones (Center on Wrongful Convictions, 2011).

> Something bizarre happened to Richard Cunningham that I never thought possible. His son attacked and murdered him in the same manner I attacked and murdered my father. I was shocked and almost unbelieving of the whole situation. What were the chances that the man defending me would

end up a victim of the same type of crime that I committed. That blew my mind more than I can put into words. Was it Karma? Irony? What?

On January 18, 2000, Steven Manning, a former Chicago police officer and FBI informant, who had been convicted of the murder of his former business partner, James Pellegrino, and sentenced to death in 1993, was exonerated. His conviction was based on the testimony of a jailhouse informant and convicted felon who was facing new charges. The FBI agents arranged to have Thomas Dye share a cell with Manning; the state's attorneys provided Dye with a tape recorder. Although Dye testified that Manning had confessed to the murders, no confession was present on the recordings. Nevertheless, Manning was convicted of the murder and sentenced to death. The prosecutors rewarded Dye by significantly reducing his sentence. Later, the Illinois Supreme Court reversed Manning's conviction, and the prosecutors dropped the charges. As such, Manning was the thirteenth man to be exonerated and released from death row in thirteen years (Center on Wrongful Convictions, 2011).

Faced with an unprecedented historical course that involved more exonerations of death-row inmates—thirteen—than executions of death-row inmates—twelve—during a period of thirteen years, Governor Ryan was forced to make a decision that would become the source of argument and debate for years to come. On January 30, 2000, Ryan declared a moratorium on executions in Illinois: "I now favor a moratorium, because I have grave concerns about our state's shameful record of convicting innocent people and putting them on death row. And, I believe many Illinois residents now feel that same deep reservation. I cannot support a system, which, in its administration, has proven to be so fraught with error and has come so close to the ultimate nightmare, the state's taking of innocent life. Thirteen people have been found to have been wrongfully convicted. How do you prevent another Anthony Porter—another innocent man or woman from paying the ultimate penalty for a crime he or she did not commit? Today, I cannot answer that question. Until I can be sure that everyone sentenced to death in Illinois is truly guilty, until I can be sure with moral certainty that no innocent man or woman is facing a lethal injection, no one will meet that fate. I am a strong proponent of tough criminal penalties, of supporting laws and programs to help police and prosecutors keep dangerous criminals off the streets. We must ensure the public safety of our citizens but, in doing so, we must ensure that the ends of justice are served" (Illinois Governor's Office, 2000).

In 2000, Governor George Ryan announced a moratorium on executions, which means he put the pause button on the machine of Death. Up until that time I had witnessed 12 men leave Death Row to be executed and another 13 men leave Death Row to go home because they were exonerated. Hope was born in my life. It occurred to me that I might actually have a future, a thought that had died when I received my death sentence. This notion forced me to do some real soul searching about who I was—who I wanted to be—and how to merge the two.

11

Moratorium and Commutation

> I began painting as a method of meditation. I also began
> to try to educate myself, psychologically, in order to try to
> understand myself. Introspection was new to me. I tried to
> figure out why certain things took place and why I did what
> I did. I read about family dynamics, dysfunctional families,
> and guilt. I read Freud and Erickson, and anything else I
> could get my hands on to help me understand myself and
> try to come to terms with my crime, which haunted me and
> compelled many of my closest relatives to loathe me to the
> point of praying for my execution.

In the wake of the moratorium, Tom Odle began a long period of self-examination as well as self-expression. The change in his perspective on
his past, and his future, was reflected in an interview he gave to *Punk
Planet*, a small, independent magazine, in an article titled, "Finding Life
on Death Row" in April 2001.

Tom begins the interview by saying, "[I]t's hard waking up every day
knowing you're going to die, especially by the hand of the state." While
the moratorium was a glimmer of hope, his future was still uncertain. To
cope, he said, "I try to stay focused on other things. I try to stay in shape,
listen to music, watch TV, paint, draw. I just try to keep very, very busy
and make sure that time passes."

His interviewer, clearly sympathetic toward Tom's situation, imagined
he would be a lot angrier. But the time Odle had already spent in prison

had taught him some valuable lessons: "Where is anger going to get you? It's not going to get you anywhere but in more trouble. . . . You have to divert your anger into other, more productive things. . . . If you're an artist, maybe you want to put your anger onto a piece of canvas or a piece of paper; or maybe you want to [physically] work it out in a workout.

"With age comes maturity. You're able to deal with your anger a lot easier. You know how to deal with it once you've gotten a little older."

When the interviewer said he found Tom's description of his day-to-day life behind bars "inspiring," Tom was quick to set him straight. "Inspiring? My life is disappearing. All of my 20s are gone. Half of my 30s are gone. Should I ever get released, I will have to start at a time when most people are settling down. I'm losing my life."

Still, the interviewer insisted, Tom was surviving "amazingly well." Tom responded, "I *have* to survive. I have to survive because if I break down and become insane, or if I break down and still stay uneducated, or let whatever talent I may have go to waste, then wouldn't you say that they win? They break me. They can keep me locked up, but mentally I'm not locked up. I *refuse* to allow them to lock me up mentally" (Staff, 2001, April).

Following the tragic death of Tom's lawyer, Richard Cunningham, who was stabbed to death by his mentally ill son on March 1, 2001, Aviva Futorian, a longtime death-row lawyer, became Tom's sole legal representative in his ongoing appeals. Futorian was an organizer for the Student Nonviolent Coordinating Committee in Mississippi during the civil-rights movement in the 1960s and cofounder of the Long Term Prisoner Policy Project, an initiative focused on prisoners' rights and Illinois prison-reform issues. She had represented other death-row inmates during the postconviction stages of their appeals.

In 2002, Futorian filed a petition for clemency from the death penalty on behalf of Thomas V. Odle in return for life without parole. Among her arguments, Futorian said:

- Odle was represented by defense counsel who did not meet the training, experience, and certification requirements of the Supreme Court amendments (Rule 714). The result was that his counsel provided seriously inadequate representation.
- They relied on an insanity defense, even though both of their mental-health experts told counsel before trial that they could not state that Odle was insane.
- Defense counsel failed to present a systematic history of the defendant's extreme emotional and physical abuse at his hearing, though the

same mental-health experts have stated that if asked, they would have stated that Odle was suffering from extreme mental and emotional disturbance.

- One of these mental-health experts strongly recommended that defense counsel obtain experts and evidence concerning parricide, which trial counsel did not do. An expert in the legal defense of parricide cases has reviewed the record and all documents relevant to the case and has concluded that Tom's trial lawyers failed to investigate and present a comprehensive history of the child abuse of Tom Odle by his parents.

Remorse, Guilt, and Shame

In a letter to the prisoner-review board, Tom asked his family to forgive him: "My parents would be enjoying their golden years and my siblings would be enjoying their lives. I live with the guilt and shame that my actions caused the deaths of my loved ones and destroyed the lives of so many others, including my own.

"I do not know any of my cousins, aunts and uncles very well. But because they are family, and some of the only family I have, I have prayed for them to find it in their hearts to forgive me and accept me as part of the family. But I never had the opportunity to talk to them about this tragedy.

"I wake every single day praying that this would have all been a dream. It still seems so unreal to me that I was capable of such an act upon my own family. If my execution would bring them back or even just one of them, I would not be asking for mercy here today.

"I am far from the troubled child and drug user that I was 17 years ago. I hope they have forgiven me and do not want to see me executed, which would only add more tragedy to my family because another member is killed."

Some of his relatives were unwavering in their demand that Odle be put to death for his crimes. But his grandmother Evelyn Eller wrote to the board in his defense:

"I know he has done a terrible thing. I believe he deserves to be punished and he should spend the rest of his life in prison. But I do not want him to die. He has gone through a lot of changes while he has been in prison. He has grown up a lot. He writes to me and always sends me birthday, Christmas and other holiday cards. I look forward to hearing from him and talking to him.

"Tom has come to mean a lot to me. I love him and I don't want him to die. Please spare his life."

Tom's petition for clemency was submitted in concert with petitions written on behalf of all Illinois death-row inmates as part of a strategy to persuade the governor to commute some or all of the death sentences. Clemency was initially denied, but ultimately, history would intercede in the life of Tom Odle.

Commutation of Death Sentences

Shortly after he declared a moratorium on executions, Governor George Ryan appointed a fourteen-member Commission on Capital Punishment to study the flawed criminal-justice system in Illinois that sentenced thirteen innocent men to death. One year later, the Illinois General Assembly approved the Capital Litigation Trust Fund to provide defense attorneys with funds to hire and pay independent investigators and forensic experts in capital-murder cases. In December 2001, the *Chicago Tribune* published a scathing expose on the coercive and illegal tactics the Chicago Police Department used to obtain confessions in seven out of every ten murder cases they reportedly solved. The 2001 article, "Cops and Confessions: Coercive and Illegal Tactics Torpedo Scores of Cook County Murder Cases" by Ken Armstrong, Steve Mills, and Maurice Possley, documents 247 murder cases in Cook County in which the police charged individuals who were in jail at the time of the murders, children, and mentally retarded suspects, based on confessions that contradict the facts of the crime and/or on DNA evidence that subsequently refuted the charges. The false confessions the police obtained in many of the cases were clearly the result of police threats, beatings, and other forms of abuse.

In March 2002, the Center on Wrongful Convictions at Northwestern University Law School released a report that documents fifteen cases in which individuals were wrongfully convicted of murder in Illinois based on their own false confessions and eleven other cases in which convictions were obtained based on the false confessions of codefendants. One month later, the Governor's Commission on Capital Punishment released its report, which proposed significant changes in the adjudication of murder cases to minimize wrongful convictions resulting from false confessions, false eyewitness testimony, and perjury by prosecution-incentivized jailhouse informants (Center on Wrongful Convictions, 2011).

As Ryan continued to wrestle with his conscience over the moratorium on executions, he was contacted by Pope John Paul II, who encouraged the governor to "take another step in the defense of life by commuting all death sentences into life in prison without the possibility of parole." Meanwhile, Chief Judge Paul Biebel, Criminal Division, Cook County

Circuit Court, appointed a special prosecutor to investigate Chicago police area 2 commander Jon Burge and a group of his detectives regarding
allegations of torture involving beatings, electric shock, and suffocation,
which were routinely conducted to obtain false confessions. Eleven individuals who were reportedly subjected to such torture were sentenced
to death and remained on death row at that time (Center on Wrongful
Convictions, 2011).

In September 2002, the *Chicago Sun-Times* published an editorial op-
posing the commutation of all death-row inmates, insisting that blanket
clemency "ignores the reality that each case must stand on its own facts."
One month later, following clemency hearings for death-row inmates,
which included emotionally charged testimony from the family members
of murder victims, the *Chicago Tribune* editorialized against the blanket
commutation of all death-row prisoners. Three weeks later, the *New York
Times* published an editorial in support of blanket clemency, proposing,
"Despite the bad publicity, Governor Ryan should do the right thing" and
commute all the death sentences to life sentences. On New Year's Eve
2002, the League of Women Voters of Illinois formally requested that
Ryan commute the sentences of all death-row inmates to life without
parole (Center on Wrongful Convictions, 2011).

On January 1, 2003, 167 men and women resided on death row in Illinois. Among these individuals were some of the most reprehensible and
violent killers in the state's 185-year history. In the view of many prosecutors throughout the state—the most outspoken being Richard Devine,
Cook County state's attorney—the executions of many of these individuals
had already been unnecessarily and illegally delayed by the moratorium
instituted in January 2000. In Devine's opinion, like that of many others
including Illinois attorney general James Ryan, the executions delayed by
the moratorium were an insult to the murdered victims and the source
of prolonged misery and grief for the families of the victims (Center on
Wrongful Convictions, 2011).

The apparent motives behind the murders committed by the 167 individuals on death row in January 2003 were diverse. The motives ranged
from personal causes, such as revenge and domestic disputes, to various
forms of criminal enterprise, including kidnapping, gang-related actions,
and robberies. Others were driven by sexually oriented motives, such as
rape and sexual torture.

Among the 167 death row inmates in January 2003 were three individuals who had committed vicious and brutal murders motivated by the
desire to kidnap a baby. In 1995, Jacqueline Williams, a black woman with

three children of her own, informed her boyfriend, Fedell Caffey, that she wanted a "light-skinned baby." In order to achieve this goal, they went to the home of a mutual friend, Debra Evans, a pregnant, white woman, and murdered her. Then, they promptly cut her nearly full-term fetus from her uterus and murdered Evans's ten-year-old daughter, Samantha, and eight-year-old-son, Joshua, who had witnessed the heinous act. Both Williams and Caffey were sentenced to death.

Similarly, in 1998, Adriana Mejia, an infertile woman without children, desperately wanted a baby. Mejia staked out an obstetrics clinic and stalked Jacinta Soto from the clinic to her home. After confirming Soto's address, Mejia recruited Gabriel Solache and Arturo DeLeon-Reyes to assist her in the abduction of the Sotos' infant daughter, Guadalupe. While Jacinta and her husband, Mariano Soto, slept, Solache, DeLeon-Reyes, and Mejia invaded their home and stabbed them to death in the presence of the baby and her three-year-old brother, Santiago. Solache was sentenced to death; Mejia and DeLeon-Reyes received life sentences.

Other notorious killers on death row at that time included some cold-blooded murderers who were motivated by money and revenge. In 1973, Henry Brisbon was convicted of the so-called I-57 murders, in which he and three accomplices lured unsuspecting motorists out of their vehicles and then robbed and murdered them on a stretch of I-57 south of Chicago. After staging a minor accident, Brisbon and his accomplices managed to stop Betty Lou Harmon and then forced her to undress. Although she managed to run away, they chased her down, and Brisbon shot her to death. Similarly, Brisbon and his crew stopped Dorothy Cerny and James Schmidt on I-57 and robbed them. Brisbon executed them with a shotgun after ordering them to "kiss your last kiss." However, Brisbon was ineligible for a death sentence at the time because he was only seventeen; his sentence was one thousand to three thousand years. But during the next ten years, he incited prison riots, wounded two death-row inmates, including John Wayne Gacy, in stabbing incidents, and was ultimately sentenced to death for the fatal stabbing of inmate Richard Morgan. During his trial for the Morgan murder, a prosecutor described Brisbon as "a walking testimonial to why we should have the death penalty."

In 2001, Luther Casteel, a forty-three-year-old truck driver, got drunk and started harassing women at JB's Pub in Elgin, Illinois, northwest of Chicago. He became so disruptive that he was thrown out of the bar. In response, he went home, shaved his head, put on military fatigues and a gas mask, and armed himself with four guns. He returned to the bar, shouted, "I'm a natural-born killer," and started shooting. Before some courageous patrons could restrain him, he killed Jeffrey Weides and Richard Bartlett and wounded sixteen others. He was convicted of two counts of first-degree murder and fifteen counts of attempted murder. According to assistant state's attorney Robert Berlin, "he has no remorse for what happened because that's the kind of person he is. . . . He's evil." After only two and a half hours of deliberation, a Kane County jury sentenced him to death.

During the first two weeks of 2003, Ryan was contacted by Nelson Mandela and Desmond Tutu, the Anglican Archbishop of South Africa. Both leaders urged him to commute the death sentences of all men and women on death row in Illinois. On January 10, 2003, Ryan pardoned four death-row prisoners, Aaron Patterson, Leroy Orange, Stanley Howard, and Madison Hobley, all of whom were convicted of murder based on confessions obtained by Chicago police detectives in the notorious area 2 police station under the supervision of commander Burge, who was fired from the Chicago Police Department in 1996 in response to multiple charges of police brutality and torture of suspects. All four denied that their confessions were voluntary but, instead, were elicited by Burge and his detectives through torture involving beatings, electric shock, and suffocation with a plastic typewriter cover.

The next day, Governor Ryan, in an internationally televised event at Northwestern University School of Law in Chicago, commuted the sentences of 163 men and women on death row to life without parole and of four others to forty years.

Of the death-row inmates whose death sentences Ryan commuted, one case is clearly unique. Nearly a third of the commuted sentences involved crimes motivated by robbery, and one fourth of the commuted sentences involved crimes motivated by sex. The others involved acts of revenge, gang-motivated murders, murders committed in relation to a kidnapping, murders that evolved out of arguments, murders of police officers, contract killings, drug-related murders, murders of fellow prison inmates, and murders with unclear motives. But only one case among the 167 individuals who were granted clemency by the governor of Illinois involved the mass murder of a family. The inmate's name is Tom Odle.

Charles Schiedel is a former deputy defender, Supreme Court Unit, Office of the State Appellate Defender of Illinois. The Office of the Appellate Defender has introduced four hundred appeals in response to death sentences in Illinois. Schiedel himself has argued thirty death-penalty cases on appeal.

According to Schiedel, "of all the social and political factors that influ-ence the death penalty, the exonerations have had the biggest impact on the death penalty in Illinois, historically. Had there not been that number of exonerations, there never would have been a moratorium." He added that the only reason Tom Odle is alive today is because thirteen men were wrongfully convicted of murder and ultimately exonerated during a period of thirteen years (personal communication, February 6, 2009).

1985 Revisited

Lawrence L. Jeckel, a forensic psychiatrist, was a key witness in Tom's murder trial. Dr. Jeckel is the court-appointed psychiatrist who conducted a pretrial psychiatric examination of Tom on December 2, 1985.

Twenty four years later, Dr. Jeckel recalled his first meeting with Tom and his impression of the young murder defendant and his crimes: "I re-member it was, obviously, a horrific crime. My lasting impression of him is being hulking and frightening. And that's in contrast to Dr. Conroe, who does not remember him in that way. It may have been that I was a younger psychiatrist, but I found him frightening. And I found the way he described how he and his brother were being chained up; there was a wild-dog quality to all of this. The sense was, here's this kid and his brother being treated like wild animals, and yet, the mother is president of the PTA. And so, there was this 'secret dog in the closet' quality to it; and very frightening to me. I was very sensitive to these things.

"So what came across to help me master my understanding of him was the psychological testing, which showed how cold and loveless and bleak he saw his world. And that made it a little easier. . . . Clearly, he was humorless and not real reachable. . . .

"So much of him talking about his brother was actually talking about himself. You know, what he couldn't talk about with regard to himself, he would talk about vis-à-vis the brother. I would take that as a displace-ment, that he really was talking about himself. But at the time, here he is post-traumatically and post-crime, he's talking in sort of a displaced manner.

"I think this was an act of rage. And that was the center of his most disturbed thinking, the rage. You know, following the rageful murders. That's really the center of his thoughts and associations, even though it's displaced onto the brother. And that seemed true, and that seemed consis-tent with everything. And if you read it that way, it's very understandable. He may lie about details, but the essence of his experience comes through, and it's pretty clear. And the same with the testing. I think the essence of his psychological universe comes through" (personal communication, March 27, 2009).

In his original report of the psychiatric evaluation he conducted in 1985, Dr. Jeckel found Tom to be sane and fit to stand trial. He also concluded that Tom's criminal history and his clinical presentation were consistent with antisocial personality disorder: "There's always the debate whether somebody's truly antisocial or do they have antisocial traits. You might look back on that. He was eighteen. Was it fully formed? Just because somebody commits a terrible, terrible murder, we would now look back, and we'd also look at chronic post-traumatic stress symptoms. There would be details, rather than just calling him antisocial.

"And actually, there are dynamics here. Yes, it's a cold rage, to say the least. But there's some affect here. And when you [the author] tell me that he's talked with you all these years later, it does not surprise me. As much as it was terrible, what was done to him and what he did to them, this was a family that did things, a family that was involved in the community. It's not like there was nothing there. There is a passion in this, a crime of passion. So, maybe if you look back on this, you see some connecting points, based on what he's told you" (personal communication, March 27, 2009).

When asked if he saw features of psychopathy in Tom, Dr. Jeckel replied: "It [the crime] has a quality of revenge. And then there's this kind of curious statement of wanting to kill the siblings because he did not want them to be hurt by the mother's death. A kind of strange empathy. So, it's very, very, very distorted, lots of sadistic, masochistic-sadistic issues. You know, it's really a rage-based thing. And that's different than psychopathy in many ways. There's a lot of affect here, looking back on it. This is a mad dog.

"I believe the fundamental thing that drove all of this was the mental abuse and the feeling that he was unprotected, the betrayal by the father. In other words, the mother was abusive, but then the father didn't protect. I believe those psychological stances are fundamental and, then, being disaffected through drugs. But I think being tormented by her and then being unprotected I think is the core. I think that's the core of the rage. Particularly the failure to be protected by the father because, in my experience, that can enrage boys more than the abuse by the mother.

"The physical abuse clearly shows the depth of it. But just the atmosphere of abuse, and then you don't know what to do and then there's no protection, there's no person to turn to. The father is passive, and he does not help the boy. And these kids, they're like mad dogs. They have no one to turn to. And the secretiveness, this stuff being kept behind four walls, it's a concentration camp is what it is" (personal communication, March 27, 2009).

Dr. Jeckel had these parting words for Tom Odle: "Tom needs to understand that that's what happened to him and how his mind dealt with it. You deadened yourself with drugs, you tried to do everything you could because you had no help. You know, I see rural people who have been in terrible situations, probably not as bad as Tom, but I go back over and over and over with them, how alone they were with it.

"This is where the betrayal of the father comes in. He was never with him. He [Tom] was all alone. And he talks about Sean, but you can see he's talking about himself here. This is what happens when boys are trapped in this kind of hellhole. You're just being double-binded. Your mother goes out, you're locked in the house, you can't talk about it. She's abusive, and the father doesn't protect you. Just one bind after another. Then that corrodes the soul and leaves you with this unbearable rage. And that's what happened.

"Now you bring your own complexities to it—your own genetics, your own development. He brings that all to the table. But that fundamental sadism of the mother, her duplicitousness, that has to be there from day 1. Because that's his mother. She had to be that way from day 1, day 2, day 3. So, she's always that way. She marries a man who somehow accommodates her . . . has his own passivities. And that evolves from age 2, age 3, on. We believe these things really start getting structured at age 2 or 3. And you can just follow it.

"The helplessness and rage just builds and builds and builds to this crescendo. And he needs to understand that he was all alone in that. And because it was hidden, how could others help him. How could others help him? If the father won't help you, then that's the bind. It just piles on top, and he had nowhere to go" (personal communication, March 27, 2009).

Henry Conroe was also a key witness in Tom's trial. Dr. Conroe, a forensic psychiatrist who was an expert witness for the defense, conducted a pretrial psychiatric examination of Tom on December 9, 1985, one week following Jeckel's evaluation.

Twenty-four years later, Dr. Conroe recalled his first meeting with Tom: "It was in the early part of my forensic career, and I had never encountered a crime of this sort. My first response was one of scientific interest, curiosity, interest, professional growth, more of a detached attitude.

"There was one thing that sort of changed my detachment even before I saw Tom. It was the DCFS records about Sean. It was really rather horrendous about him being chained and locked out of the refrigerator. And, somehow I found myself, in a bizarre way, even before I saw Tom, feeling . . . I hate to use the word *sympathy* but feeling a glimmer of empathy.

"So, I went from this detachment to feeling that something was amiss here. Obviously, these things don't happen in a vacuum. Was this the smoking gun? Not so much what caused him to do it that day, but was it the tip of the iceberg, this type of behavior, by putting a child on a chain. And I guess he [Sean] had been diagnosed with psychosocial dwarfism. So, professionals had seen him and thought something was quite amiss, even though it was a middle-class family, father worked for the phone company. Seemed like a regular Midwestern family, but under the surface there were some pretty dark things that were happening.

"So that shifted me from looking at this like a butterfly on a pin to feeling perhaps really drawn in and feeling that I could show some empathy, not sympathy, but empathy. Then, when I saw him, in the Cook County Jail, it was a rather unique experience. And unique in the sense, compared to experiences I've had subsequently, when I've interviewed people who have murdered or raped. And I don't think I've experienced it again. As he [Tom] was relating these incidents, I felt nauseated. Now, I've had people tell me about some very terrible things they've done. And he wasn't cold when he said it. In fact, he was somewhat scared, somewhat depressed, tearful at times. But it was the methodical manner in which he committed these murders, including his siblings, people who he said he cared for and probably did to some degree. But yet, it wasn't as if a voice was telling him to do this, such as a hallucination. It was a playing-out of this whole thing. It was something I had never experienced before and have not really experienced since.

"I felt that maybe because he was in the Cook County Jail, he was scared. Sometimes there is a bravado that a defendant will show. He certainly didn't show that. And I felt he was like a young trembling kid. Then, I felt some sympathy for him, but at the same time, I felt revulsion at what he did. But I didn't see any evidence of psychosis, obviously. There was some evidence of mood disorder but not to the level that I could use it for an insanity defense. That's why I said I couldn't really reach a conclusion. On the other hand, I didn't see it as being purely psychopathic or purely antisocial. It seemed that there was a darkness in this family that had affected him. He articulated it in the best way possible, and I guess I used the term *borderline personality* to try to conceptualize it. I don't know if that's 100 percent accurate.

"In some ways, the dehumanized ways in which the brother was treated were very similar to the way in which he, Tom, dispatched his family. Perhaps that's what I was trying to convey to the jury, and unsuccessfully, because he got death, and understandably. It was a horrendous crime. Trying to get people to feel sympathy or empathy is an uphill battle. But that was my hope, one way or the other, by putting it in some context. I didn't want to blame the victims. That's always a danger. But something like this, that is so out of the ordinary. It wasn't like he just went on a rampage and dispatched them by going in and shooting them. Rather, it was a step-by-step sequence, interrupted by smoking some pot and going out with friends. It would be very hard for a jury to feel either sympathy or empathy for someone like that" (personal communication, January 23, 2009).

Dr. Conroe was asked, why, in his opinion, is Tom Odle still alive today? "That is complicated because of my philosophy regarding the death penalty. I'm opposed to the death penalty. And I think that Tom . . . clearly was guilty, guilty in the sense of he's the one who did it. It wasn't some drifter who came in and did it. Tom was the guy who did it. It's made difficult by my belief that, and maybe this is going to haunt me in future trials, but it should not be the work of the government to execute people. That's my personal philosophy. It's not as a forensic psychiatrist. It's as a citizen.

"We know of incidents in which people confessed to crimes that they didn't commit. In Tom's case, was this guy just evil? OK, he did something evil, but when we look at it, this didn't happen in a vacuum. Certainly, him eventually receiving a life sentence, I have no problem with that. But should the government be in the business of executing people, I'm opposed to that. And that's something I have to be very careful about.

"I can see that Tom's case is very different from those other thirteen death-row inmates who were exonerated. It shows there are a lot of problems with the death penalty. I'm not going to say he [Tom] just made a mistake, because it's obviously more than that. But . . . I think our government can show compassion and also have justice, too. I mean, justice by locking him away for the rest of his life but also showing compassion by not executing him" (personal communication, January 23, 2009).

Dr. Conroe made reference to his 1985 report on Carolyn Odle's sadism: "You know, kids model their behavior on their parents. And as a parent of three boys, there are times when I feel frustrated, but I found it very difficult to sympathize or empathize with her. To say that Sean was so unmanageable that [you] chain him to a bed—it's sort of outside the realm of being able to understand, just as it's outside the realm of understanding what Tom did. You know, this wasn't as if she lost it and slapped him. Rather, it was very methodical.

"And I'm not saying that A led to B, but when that is allowable in a house, then the usual boundaries of civility and treatment of other people are somehow or other impaired. You know, again, it had the veneer of a regular middle-class house, a hardworking, middle-class family. But when there are those types of things that are permissible, where they're allowed and they're sanctioned, somebody vulnerable like Tom [will be affected]. If you're sadistic toward your own kid, then his sadism toward his own family seems to lower the barriers. For example, what he did with his sister. He played sort of a game with her, sort of cat and mouse. Well, you can say that's evil. But why would he do that? And somehow when sadism is permissible, then the bar is very low in a household like that. Now, there are clearly other households with abuse in which this doesn't happen. But we're talking about Tom and his vulnerability as one factor that lowers the bar. Once again, it's always a danger in blaming the victim, but it's so outside the realm of usual behavior. His sadism toward his own family is more understandable" (personal communication, January 23, 2009).

Dr. Conroe reflected on Tom's killing of all his siblings as well as his parents: "I guess I see this act as total destruction of the family, including himself, because he knew he would be captured. He didn't run away to Mexico. I think that certain individuals get into a state of nihilism, where they're just going to take down the whole world with them, including themselves. I understand it as bringing down the whole world, bringing down the entire family, because at that time, he probably knew that his life had essentially ended.

"I think he felt that his life had essentially ended when he was thrown out of the house. That was the abandonment. And then his life, it was over when he killed his two parents. At that point, he just brought down the whole structure. I think it's hard for us to understand because most of us would say, 'Oh my God, what have I done.' But people in this state of nihilism . . . they're just going to take everything down with them, including themselves.

"I do remember him, and I don't remember all of them [criminal defendants] like this. I think what's different is that he didn't really try to defend himself or excuse himself. I think he told me it was like seeing a movie, and it was like he was taking me through it scene by scene. And, you know, I knew where it was going, but there was something about that. He was a slight kid who seemed scared. And he was tearful, but they weren't tears to 'feel sorry for me.' That's why he didn't seem sociopathic or antisocial. But, obviously there are those elements.

"Obviously, what he did was cold-blooded, but I didn't sense the cold-bloodedness. I didn't feel that he thought, 'I really gave those m-f-s what they deserved,' or anything like that. It's sort of interesting and sort of confusing. You want to condemn this guy, because, OK, you did your parents, but why your siblings? And I didn't feel that he was trying to get sympathy from me or anything like that, because that falls flat. There was some genuine, maybe, remorse or at least some remorse for what he did. But yet, he did it, and the way in which he did it says something about it, too.

"It's interesting that it wasn't until his death sentence was commuted that he tried to find some sort of meaning in what happened or tried to make sense of what happened. Not when death was facing him, but when life was facing him" (personal communication, January 23, 2009).

> For nearly 18 years I had simply pushed everything to the back of my mind, while lifting weights, playing basketball, getting drunk, watching TV, and listening to the radio. It was time to face my fears and demons. I slowly dissected my actions and my life. This book is about my final stage of analysis, which now leads me on to a more progressive life. I've recently graduated from college and am looking forward to further education as much as circumstances allow, because educated people make educated decisions, and never again do I want to find myself in this or any similar situation.

12

Atonement

In 2013, Tom Odle will turn forty-seven. He has spent twenty-eight years in prison, more than half of his life. Seventeen of those years were spent on death row. He has developed a powerful build after years of weight training and basketball. He still wears his hair long, similar to the look he had as a teenager. He keeps his mustache and goatee neatly trimmed. His blue eyes are clear. They tell you that they've seen a lot, a lot they would like to forget. But they are intelligent and thoughtful eyes. The ability to learn is a freedom he still has, and he has gone to great lengths to exercise that freedom.

As a result of the fact that he has spent his entire adult life in maximum-security prisons, he has had very few of the interpersonal and social experiences that would enable him to develop into a responsible adult. Despite the increased self-awareness and insight he has gained from the self-exploration required to write this book, and the educational opportunities he has pursued within the prison system, he remains a work in progress. Given his history of conduct disorder and antisocial personality disorder, combined with the fact that he committed one of the most horrific family mass murders in U.S. history, he will always be a work in progress.

Tom's maternal grandmother, Evelyn Eller, died in 2006. He mourned her death for nearly a year. Through correspondence and phone calls, they had become quite close over the years, despite his crimes. He still gets occasional communications from other family members, cousins mainly. The family connections remain very important to him.

Natural Life without Parole

Twenty-eight years in prison have given him plenty of time to reflect on his life and circumstances. During an interview on Christmas Day 2006, he stated that if he had not spent his entire adult life in prison, "going the way I was going, I'd probably be dead. I'd just be dead . . . drug overdose, drinking and driving, being drunk and drowning, you know something like that." He imagined it would have been a violent death but nothing involving a crime.

He was still uncertain as to what pushed him over the edge that fateful November day in 1985. "I made it to the army and I got pulled back. I made it to Kentucky where I was working at a renovation company and had my own place, and I ended up getting pulled back home. 'Come home, we'll work this out. We want you here.' I was always looking for approval. I was always looking for that family that I idealized but never had. Every time it was offered to me, I took it. It still didn't work out. I still held that hope, got away, but I kept getting pulled back. I kept allowing myself to be pulled back.

"I just know I'd had enough. It's like this thing just chose me. I feel like it chose me, not me choosing it. Why this particular action took place, why I chose this day or this particular time, I don't know. Before it was always my mother telling me, 'You gotta get out, you gotta get out,' and this was my father telling me also to leave. And it hurt. My dad was actually taking her side. Maybe that was the one thing that was too much: My dad taking the side with her. He had rarely done that before. He was like my advocate, the quiet one, I mean he let things go on. . . .

"I had enough, and everybody was adding to the problems, nobody seemed to want to help. Nobody wanted to solve the problems. It was always, 'Solve the problems by violence,' and after you got the beating, the problem was still there. It made more problems.

"It just continues from generation to generation: the abuse, the neglect, the violence. You know, if that's how you're raised, then that's all you are going to know. You think that is the right way to raise your child. You don't know any better, so you pass it on to your children, and they pass it on to their children. I recognize that this is wrong. I'd like to be able to pass on my information and to be sure the cycle has stopped; that this is how you act. I want someone to be proud to say, 'That's my dad,' and not deny me."

He remembers vividly that in the immediate aftermath of the crime, he had difficulty believing that it actually happened. That was one of the reasons he made his infamous request to phone his father from jail.

"It was like I was looking at myself, outside looking in. It was me doing everything, but it wasn't me. It was like somebody else, like it really wasn't happening. Like a dream or something. I didn't think it was real. I didn't actually think I did what was going on. Not me, 'cause I'm not cut from that cloth. You know, I'm not a naturally violent person. I wasn't a violent person. I got into a few fights, but it was all growing-up stuff. I never carried guns and knives, I never did violent crimes. I never did things like that.

"It didn't hit me until I was in the courtroom. When I was arraigned, I went into the shakes. I don't know if it was because I was scared, but something. I kind of lost it. When he was reading the charges, it finally sunk in just exactly what happened. And that was four or five days later. I just remember sitting there shaking, I couldn't stop shaking and I couldn't walk. I was just freaking out, and that's when it dawned on me that it really happened. I'm really in jail. I'm really in this orange jumpsuit. I'm really in a courtroom. This is no fantasyland, this is actually real.

"When it first hit me that I'd been arrested, and realized what I'd done, I had a reoccurring dream. I was going home, and they [my family] would come around the corner. They were all sewn up from where they got cut. They wouldn't say anything to me. They would just follow me to my room. Then, as I lay on the bed and without saying anything to me, they would attack me. But I would always wake up before they attacked me."

When he arrived on death row, "I was scared to death." But after he took up residence on death row, "they seemed to be more scared of my crime and of me than I was of them, because they had seen me on TV."

Tom would discover there was more to coping with life on death row than dealing with the day-to-day restrictions and regulations. It would take years for him to confront the real issues that were gnawing away inside him.

"The moratorium really started making me deal with the bully that was chasing me around. I really could be a better person. It's hard to think about certain things when you're in a hopeless situation. Without hope you have no light. Everything is dark. I didn't want my grandmother to have to put me in the ground, too. It [the moratorium] took a lot of weight off of my shoulders, and it took a lot of weight off of my family's shoulders. They had to carry that burden with me.

"I decided that I couldn't keep running from what I did. It's always gonna be there, it's always going to follow me. That bully is always gonna follow you, always gonna chase you, beat you down, and take all of whatever you got. It takes your emotions. And you gotta say, 'You're not going to do this to me anymore. You're not gonna play with me.' So you just gotta take the bricks down out of the bully. Look at it, deal with it, say, 'I did this.' Analyze it. You take this in. If you feel you are comfortable enough that you can deal with this, then you can walk with it. Not just take it, but you've got to walk with it. If you feel you can walk with it, then you can take on something else until there is no more bully following you. Now you're just walking, nothing chasing you, you're just walking. You've got a wagon with some baggage in it, but you're doing the walking, you're not running. You're walking."

Of course, the self-evaluation was hard. But it was also healing. The healing process gave him a new range of emotions to deal with. "Remorse? It's not a strong enough word. Remorseful just means you're sorry. I'm ashamed. I'm embarrassed. No person should do this. It's hard living knowing what I've done. It's deeper. It's a constant ache.

"I started reading books about parricide, and I could see myself in all these different stories. I didn't feel so alone. I could see somebody else did this, somebody else had been through this. This is not just *my* case. There are a lot of us. And when I started seeing myself in a lot of the different cases, it made things easier to take. I had more insight. That's why, when I started reading these things, that's why I wrote to you. You know, I said, 'I read this, is this really true?' That helped me tremendously."

Like all those facing life in prison, Tom copes by holding out hope that one day, he will be given the opportunity to leave his cell for good.

Aviva Futorian is still Tom Odle's attorney. She joined Tom's legal team when his lawyer, the late Richard "Dick" Cunningham, asked her to be co-counsel in 1997 during his appeals. "Tom's postconviction appeal was denied, and so it was Dick's job to go into federal court at that point, which is the next stage. Dick went into federal court and asked for a stay of proceedings so that he could go back into state court and ask to do a second postconviction, which is very seldom allowed. That's when Dick asked me if I wanted to be co-counsel, which I certainly did.

"Dick had developed a very close feeling for Tom. Dick was an alcoholic in recovery and had not had a drink for thirteen years. Tom had gotten a ticket [prison-rule violation] for making hooch in his cell, and Dick felt that Tom was a very addictive personality, because Dick was, and he recognized the signs. So he had a close feeling for Tom and used to talk to him about that a lot. As you know, Dick died, tragically, in 2001. He was killed by his son, who was mentally ill.

"Dick was requesting an evidentiary hearing on the issue of mitigation. We felt that both his trial attorney and his first postconviction attorney did a very poor job providing mitigation to the death penalty. I think evidence of his family background might have given him a new sentencing hearing and resulted in what would have been a mandatory life sentence, rather than the death penalty.

"Now, I'm probably not very objective about it. I felt so sure, given his excellent mitigation, that any court would have ordered a new sentencing hearing. But the courts are very tough on that, particularly since Tom had already had a first chance at a postconviction, a postconviction which had been handled by an attorney who was very able but had a personal dislike of Tom. It was very, very strange. When Dick, who was Tom's second postconviction attorney, contacted this first postconviction attorney and asked him for a statement indicating that he had not done a thorough job; what he wrote back and said for the record was that he found Tom to be a very narcissistic person. Now, that may have been, but he was supposed to be helping Tom. He was Tom's defense attorney. He was supposed to comment on his own performance, not on Tom's" (personal communication, February 3, 2009).

As to Tom's change of heart and perspective following the moratorium, Futorian said, "It made him feel good, but I don't think it changed the fact that he thought he was going to die." She also agreed with Charles Schiedel, Supreme Court Unit, Office of State Appellate Defender, in his view that if thirteen men had not been wrongfully convicted of murder, sentenced to death, and subsequently exonerated of their crimes, Tom Odle would not be alive today.

"One day Tom said something very nice to me. I had told him, 'If you have any questions or you want to talk about any of the legal issues regarding your case, ask me.' And he said, 'I gotta tell you something. Another inmate came up to me the other day and asked if my attorney was doing this or doing that, and I kept saying, 'I don't know.' He said, 'That's bad; you've got to find out—but wait a minute, who *is* representing you?' Tom said, 'Cunningham and Futorian.' And the other guy said, 'Oh shit, you don't have to worry then.' Tom said, 'I felt so good.' Of course, I did, too. It was a very nice thing for him to tell me. In a way, he was a perfect client. He's come a long way since then, and I think it really began when he got in contact with you" (personal communication, February 3, 2009).

It's no accident that Futorian has taken on what is certainly a difficult case: "I've become involved with prisoner reform. I started a group called the Long Term Prisoner Policy Project, which was funded by the George Soros Foundation. Then we became part of the John Howard Association, which is the only prisoner-reform group in the State of Illinois. So, it's through the Long Term Prisoner Policy Project and the John Howard Association that I've been working on the issue of transfers, because long-term prisoners are not eligible to transfer to medium-security prisons, regardless of their behavior.

"I'm also very much involved in what's called the C Number Campaign, which has nothing to do with Tom directly. The C Number prisoners are those prisoners who were sentenced for crimes committed before 1978, which was before the State of Illinois got rid of parole, so they're still eligible for parole.

"These are some of the best-behaved prisoners in the correctional system because they were in prison when the prisons still focused on rehabilitation. So, they had interesting education programs and jobs, et cetera. Some of these inmates are incredibly rehabilitated. But now we have a prisoner-review board, which is the group that decides on their parole every year, that isn't concerned with rehabilitation. So we are trying to change that in different ways: changing the rules, changing the membership in the prisoner-review board. The prisoner-review board is also the group that recommends clemency to the governor, so to that extent it is relevant to Tom. At this point, the John Howard Association would like to bring back parole to Illinois" (personal communication, February 3, 2009).

Many books and articles have been written about those who spend their lives behind bars, and there is a consensus about the general character of lifers. Most develop a realistic assessment of their situation, an assessment that reflects a mature sense of coping and adaptation. Prison life is all they have, and so they make the most of it. They adopt the others who share their fate, life imprisonment, as family. They make the most of the opportunities prison life provides to create the most livable and decent life possible. They try to avoid trouble that would lead to losing the few privileges they have. And they try to use the insight they have gained from their years of incarceration to steer other inmates toward better lives. In this context, Tom Odle has become a model prisoner.

In an interview in 2009, he examined the life he has made for himself: "I've been here for the last six years [Lawrence Correctional Center], following my seventeen years on death row at Menard and Pontiac and a brief stint at Stateville. And I've had a job for over three years. I do the floors. I strip floors, wax floors, make the floors nice and shiny. That's my job, and I'm sure that when I go to another facility they're going to look at my record and say, 'Okay, he knows how to do floors. Put him on floor care'" (personal communication, July, 17, 2009).

He has also worked as a porter. One of the porter's jobs is to keep peace on the wing. "You sweep, mop, dust the floors; you're kind of an intermediary between the bullshit on the wing and the correctional officers. So, if an officer's having a bad day—we all have bad days—he may not want to deal with things. So he may go out into the front hall all day or go into the foyer. I try to resolve everything I can on the wing. He may need something; I get it. I take care of it.

"If it's something I can't take care of, then I talk to him. I'll tell him, 'The dude's got this problem,' and he'll either say, 'Tell him this or that,' or he'll go do it himself, personally. You know, you just become an intermediary, you kinda cut down bullshit between the inmates and the officer. It keeps the officer off the wing so he ain't yelling at people. He's off the wing, and I take care of it" (personal communication, July 17, 2009).

Tom recently earned an associate's degree. He's the first and only former death-row inmate among the 167 death-row inmates whose sentences were commuted to achieve a college degree. When introduced at his graduation, it was announced, "Tom isn't supposed to be with us today, because he was supposed to be executed." But he has nearly exhausted the available educational opportunities. It is a source of frustration that he cannot use his time to improve his mind. "Libraries were shut down, you know, to cut staff. They took away a lot of different things. As a result, the inmates stay in their cells more of the time. When you put somebody in a cell more of the time, he or she has more time to think. You don't have a book to read because you can't go to the library. So what is your mind going to do? Your mind's going to dwell on hatred, revenge, bitterness, and depression.

"In the lower-level facilities, like levels 2 to 4, you have access to college education, and the libraries are open. You can't just put people in cells and leave them. You've got to get them educated. Educated people make educated decisions. So if you send an educated person back to the world, he's going to make educated decisions and hopefully, [be] educated enough that he won't land in the penitentiary again. If he's had enough of this, he'll be able to do whatever he needs to do to sustain his life by legal means" (personal communication, July 17, 2009).

Tom has had ten different cellmates since he left death row. "When I get a new cellie, I'm always the one who's got more time, so I've got to explain things to him. He's the one getting educated. 'You do these things, you don't do those things.' And, he lives downstairs, and I live upstairs, on the top bunk. I'm up here, and he's down there, we talk every now and then and watch TV" (personal communication, July 17, 2009).

Tom has adopted the "go along to get along" philosophy that is characteristic of so many dealing with life in prison. He avoids trouble. But he does not hesitate to speak his mind when it comes to encouraging others to stay out of prison for good.

"I try to talk to some of these kids who make light of being locked up here for six months, and I can't let it slide. The other day, we were talking in political-science class about political views. One guy said that he didn't believe in the death penalty. He said that he believes a guy should get natural life because he will be tormented for the rest of his life. I'm in this class. He doesn't know I'm in this class. He doesn't know my sentence.

"Guys who know me were looking at me . . . to set him straight, to challenge him. But I didn't. Instead, I pulled him aside. I didn't want to do it in front of the class. I pulled him aside as we were leaving. I said, 'You don't think that doing six months here in a penitentiary is suffering? How much time do you think a person must do to suffer?' I said, 'Anytime you're not out there with your family, anytime you're locked up in this facility, *is* suffering. What do you consider suffering?' He just looked at me like a target. I didn't tell him that I'm doing natural life. That wasn't the point. I wanted to know . . . what he considered suffering to be, because apparently he's not suffering. If he was, he wouldn't have said that. So, the time he's doing is useless. He hasn't learned his lesson. He will be back.

"You don't understand suffering until you've done it. You have to do time. Each person is different. For one person, it may be two years before he says I can't go back, I can't do it, I have to get my life right. For another guy, it may take twenty years before he finally gets it through his head, 'I've had enough. I can't do this anymore. You know, this is not the life I picked; this is not the life for me.'

"In comes a new guy, and you hear him talking. They talk loud because they want other people to hear them. I'll say, 'Excuse me, young brother, can I ask you a question? Why aren't you out there raising your kids? Why aren't you out there keeping your kids from doing what you've done? What kind of example are you setting for your kids by being in here?' They all get quiet.

"How fun do you think it is to come to prison to find your culture? This is the killer part. Many black men who come to prison investigate the black culture because they have time—how blacks were treated, historically, where they come from. I think that's wonderful. I think everybody should know where they come from. Know your own culture and ancestry. But why do you say that you'll go back out there and sell drugs to the same people that you claim to be a part of. Why do you go back out there and use a gun that you don't know how to shoot and inadvertently kill a child two blocks away. They don't have an answer.

"How long is it going to take before you finally realize that you can change your life right now, before it's too late? Because you're going to mess around until you end up like me. I'm getting ready to complete twenty-eight years. I've spent seventeen of them on death row waiting to die every day. I was there knowing I'm going to die. I'm going to be stretched out on a gurney, in a Jesus Christ pose, in front of strangers.

"They just look at me like I'm an ass. They don't fully comprehend the different aspects of life, that they could change simply by doing so. I tell them, 'You don't want to mop that floor? Don't tell me there aren't any jobs out there. You feel the jobs are beneath you. That's all it is. I'll clean that toilet with a smile, I'll mop that floor, I'll shine that damned chrome, I'll do whatever I have to do to get that check, to keep from coming to this penitentiary. There's no job beneath me. But they don't get it. They like that quick 'easy' money. They like what JZ is doing on TV and try to live his life.

"But when you come to prison, you're broke. Where's your money now? Where's all that money you had? You were making thousands of dollars every day, but now, you can't even afford a TV, you can't even buy a pair of boxers. Where's your money? You're out there for six months making thousands of dollars, and you're locked up for the next twenty years. You better hope that the money is worth twenty years of your life. But when I'm telling them this, they get quiet. I don't know if they start thinking or they feel sorry for me. I hope they start thinking. But there are some guys who just have to be so cool and so tough. They say, 'I'll keep doing what I do until I die.' It's sad, it's really sad.

"At what point do you say, 'I don't mind coming back to this prison.' At what point do you say, 'Alright, prison ain't so bad.' I don't like living in a cell with another man and smelling his shit. If that ain't enough reason, what else do you need? You don't know how lucky you are. That makes me very irate because I know they're going to continue to offend. I know this.

"Most guys who commit crimes like mine, murder, it's like a heat of the moment kind of thing, and it's over. It's spent, unless you're a true psychopath. It ain't going to happen again. Whereas these drug dealers are habitual offenders. When they go in front of the judge, they come to the joint. How many chances did they get before coming to the joint? You know, on the street, selling dope, possession, manufacture, possession, OK, you're going to go to the joint now. They go to the joint for possession, they get back out, they go back to court: possession, possession, distribution. You know, I can't see why the courts are sending people to the joint and then letting them out to offend again, instead of letting the people out who are going to try to do better, to contribute to society. That's my opinion" (personal communication, July 17, 2009).

Final Reflections

In 2012, Tom was transferred to the Dixon Correctional Center. "When I first started this project, I thought it would be interesting to see just what I could remember from my childhood, and I didn't think it would be so much. But after sitting down and thinking about everything, I was able to remember a lot more than I thought possible. It's like a roller-coaster ride for me because I can recall all the bad memories and some of the good ones. The bad ones make me sad because they felt they had to treat me that way, and I'm sorry for my mother for having to live the way she did with all that anger. But when you're a little kid, you don't understand what is going on. All you're looking for is some love and understanding from the people around you, not threats of violence, beatings, and being told you're nothing and that your mother regrets having you. When I was younger, I always wondered what it was that I did wrong, but as I grow older, I see that it was her problem, not mine. I do, however, get sad wishing I could sit down and speak with her now at my age in an effort to gain insight to what really made her act the way she did.

"I long for my family and am saddened that what took place had to happen. I wish I could see them again and talk with them, apologize for my actions and hope that I am forgiven. I've had some sleepless nights just going over my past life with all the stuff done to me and all the stuff I have done to others. A lot of people did not deserve what I did to them, like using girls for sex and robbing people who worked hard for what they had just to have me come along and take it from them. Sometimes, I wonder if I was that very bad person some people were talking about during my trial. I wonder what those people really think of me now, the people I hurt. I have thought about trying to find some of them and apologize, but that would only bring up bad memories. It would help me, but would it help them? I don't know.

"I see that I have done a lot of wrong things in my life and am beginning to see why I went the way I did. So, once again, I go back to if I had just a little love and understanding as a child and if my mother had had a little love and understanding during her life, then she would not have been the way she was during her life. I wish I could go back in time and change some of the things I did and use more wisdom in the choices I made. But I can't.

"This project has helped me find some of the answers, but there are still some that can never be answered. And it is painful and a deep sorrow for my soul to live through some of these memories. Several years ago, I was sent to Pinckneyville Correctional Center, which is very close to my hometown, and there are people employed from that area. What got to me was how many people remembered and had the question of why, even though it had been nearly twenty years. Officers would come to my door and ask why I did what I did. And there were people I went to school with who just asked me if I was OK. And then there were the people who thought I should have been executed. I was so happy to not only be in a medium-security facility but happy to be in my area where at least I could feel like I was at home. But those staff members let me know in not so many words that I could never go home again. That was a bitter pill to swallow because it was like they let the air out of my sails by putting me in segregation and shipping me to another facility within one week of arriving there. That let me know that even though I cannot get past this, there are a lot of other people that are deeply affected, and I will never be seen as anyone other than a monster, regardless of who I am or who I become in the future. But regardless of what people think of me, I have to do this for me, and in the process, I hope that I can prevent other kids who are in the situation I felt I was in from doing what I did. It has made me determined to better myself and find the answers I need.

"I don't believe that my whole purpose for being was to commit this crime and go to death row to die. There has to be more to it to give me hope . . . to be involved in a church, to tell my story, make myself available to youth, to let them know what I've been through, and let them know that they could tell me anything. I'm not gonna let you down. I'll do my best to help you.

"It's been a hell of a life, a hell of a road, and I hope nobody else has to go down a road like this. My story could be used as a teaching tool if someone else comes down this road, if they feel this is the only thing they have left. Options. When you're young and you get involved in drugs, you are really not aware of the world. Life is so narrow, and you're not really thinking about tomorrow or looking for opportunities. You think, 'I've got to resolve this right here, right now.' It's a little picture as compared to the big picture. Be proud of it cause it's the only one you get" (personal communication, December 21, 2012).

Epilogue

On March 9, 2011, the death penalty was abolished in the State of Illinois. From 1977, when the death penalty was reinstated, to 2000, when the moratorium on executions was instituted, 298 men and women were sentenced to death in Illinois. Of those 298 individuals who were convicted of murder and sentenced to death by Illinois courts, 12 were executed, and 20 were ultimately exonerated. Thirteen were exonerated prior to the moratorium, and 7 were exonerated after the moratorium was initiated. This exoneration rate of nearly 7 percent is higher than any other state with a death-penalty statute on the books (Center on Wrongful Convictions, 2011). Due to this alarming exoneration rate, combined with the risk of executing an innocent person, Governor Pat Quinn, a former death-penalty advocate, signed the bill to abolish the death penalty that had been approved by the Illinois legislature two months earlier. The new law took effect on July 1, 2011.

As previously mentioned, Tom Odle was transferred to the Dixon Correctional Center of the Illinois Department of Corrections in 2012. He survived seventeen years on death row, and his life was spared by the moratorium. Following the abolition of the death penalty and his transfer to the penitentiary where he will likely remain for the rest of his life, Tom reflected on the difference between the death penalty and life without parole. His is a rare perspective. Very few people have directly experienced both sides of this controversial issue. In January, 2013, he spoke with me about his future.

"The realization of where my life is going to end up is very depressing. I see individuals who have done many years lying in beds, praying for death to come and take them away from prison. They're in their seventies and eighties with terminal illnesses. They're all alone. Nobody writes. Nobody visits. And who would? They're old and dying. They came in here as young men, just like I did. Their lives were spent living in a cage because of something they did when they were teenagers. Like me, they were deemed pieces of human garbage who should never inhabit the realm of free society again. But they always hang on to a sliver of hope that one day they can be free, again.

Am I going to end up in one of those beds with a terminal illness, just like them? It makes me want to break down and get on my knees and just cry. Not cry for them, but cry for how I've ruined my life and the lives of many others. I never really entertained what my life would be like if I had to spend my whole life in prison, until now. Now, I'm staring at it every single day. I was talking with a guy the other day who was on death row with me, and I asked him a question.

"A young kid kills his family because he lashes out in the only form of retaliation he knows—violence. He goes to death row and spends nearly twenty years waiting to die. He's prepared to die. But they let him off death row. Now, he sits around waiting to die in prison, always looking out the window at what he can never have, never touching or experiencing life, just enduring life until the body finally gives out—hanging on to hope that deep down he knows will never come. But he hangs on, anyway, because he has to, so he can get out of bed and function. Now, doesn't the death penalty seem more like a release or a gift than life in prison?'

"We both looked at each other for a long time and dropped our heads because it's wrong to pray for death, isn't it?"

REFERENCES

INDEX

References

Allen, S. (1985, November 22). To the editor. *The Register-News*.

American Association for Protecting Children. (1988). *Highlights of official child neglect and abuse reporting: 1986*. Denver, CO: American Humane Association.

American Psychiatric Association. (2000). *Diagnostic and statistical manual of mental disorders*. (4th ed., text rev). Washington, DC: American Psychiatric Association.

Armstrong, K., & Mills, S. (1999, November 15). Inept defenses cloud verdict. *Chicago Tribune*. Retrieved from http://articles.chicagotribune.com/1999-11-15/news/chi-991115deathillinois2_1_sentencing-hearing-bernon-howery-earl-washington

Armstrong, K., Mills, S., & Possley, M. (2001, December 16). Cops and confessions: Coercive and illegal tactics torpedo scores of Cook County murder cases. *Chicago Tribune*. Retrieved from https://www.chicagotribune.com/news/watchdog/chi-011216confession,0,1748927.story?page=4

Bohm, R. (1999). *Deathquest: An introduction to the theory and practice of capital punishment in the United States*. Cincinnati, OH: Anderson.

Boots, D. P., & Heide, K. M. (2006). Parricides in the media: A content analysis of available reports across cultures. *International Journal of Offender Therapy and Comparative Criminology, 50*, 418–445.

Callarman, J. (1985, November 11). In slayings of Mt. Vernon family 18-year-old in jail without bond. *The Register-News*, 1A–2A.

Center on Wrongful Convictions, Northwestern University School of Law. (2011). Retrieved from http://www.law.northwestern.edu/wrongfulconvictions

City of Mt. Vernon, Illinois. (2011). Retrieved from http://www.mtvernon.com

Death Penalty Information Center. (2011). Retrieved from http://www.deathpenaltyinfo.org/

Duwe, G. (2004). The patterns and prevalence of mass murder in twentieth-century America. *Justice Quarterly, 21*, 729–762.

"Electric Chair, The." (2010). *Capital Punishment U.K.* Retrieved from http://www.capitalpunishmentuk.org/chair.html

Ewing, C. P. (2001). Parricide. In G. F. Pinard & L. Pagani (Eds.), *Clinical assessment of dangerousness: Empirical contributions* (pp. 181–194). New York: Cambridge University Press.

Finding life on death row. (2001, April). *Punk Planet*.

Ford v. Wainwright, 477 U.S. 399. (1986). Retrieved from http://supreme.justia.com/us/477/399/case.html

Fox, D. (1985, November 11). Neighbors shocked by mass slaying. *Southern Illinoisan*, p. 5.

———. (1985, November 12). Teen admits he killed family. *Southern Illinoisan*, p. 1.

Furman v. Georgia, 408 U.S. 238. (1972). Retrieved from http://supreme.justia.com/cases/federal/us/408/238.case.html

Greene, Bob. (1983). *American beat*. New York: Atheneum.

Gregg v. Georgia, 428 U.S. 153. (1976). Retrieved from http://laws.findlaw.com/us/428/153.html

Hawkins, J. D., Herrenkohl, T. L, Farrington, D. P., Brewer, D., Catalano, R. F., Harachi, T. W., & Cothern, L. (2000, April). Predictors of youth violence. *Juvenile Justice Bulletin*. Washington DC: Office of Juvenile Justice and Delinquency Prevention, U.S. Department of Justice.

Heide, K. M. (1989). Parricide: Incidence and issues. *The Justice Professional, 4*, 19–41.

——. (1992). *Why kids kill parents: Child abuse and adolescent homicide*. Columbus: The Ohio State University Press.

——. (1995). Dangerously antisocial youths who kill their parents. *Journal of Police and Criminal Psychology, 10*, 10–14.

——. (1999). *Young killers: The challenge of juvenile homicide*. Thousand Oaks, CA: Sage.

Illinois Coalition to Abolish the Death Penalty. (2011). Retrieved from http://www.icadp.org

Illinois Governor's Office. (2000). Governor Ryan declares moratorium on executions, will appoint commission to review capital punishment system. Retrieved from http://www.illinois.gov/pressreleases

Leggett, V. L. (2000). Parricidal familicide. In P. H. Blackman, V. L. Leggett, B. L. Olson, & J. P. Jarvis (Eds.), *The varieties of homicide and its research: Proceedings of the 1999 meeting of the homicide research working group* (pp. 196–210). Washington, DC: Federal Bureau of Investigation.

Leyton, E. (1990). *Sole survivor: Children who murder their families*. New York: Pocket Books.

Mailer, N. (1979). *The Executioner's Song*. Boston: Little, Brown.

Minton, M., & Snyder, R. (1985, November 13). Members of slain family laid to rest. *The Register-News*, p. 1-A.

People of the State of Illinois vs. Thomas V. Odle, No. 85-CF-223. (1986). Report of the proceedings of the trial in the Circuit Court of the Second Judicial Circuit, Jefferson County, Illinois.

Perez, C. M., & Widom, C. S. (1994). Childhood victimization and long-term intellectual and academic outcomes. *Child Abuse and Neglect, 18*, 617–633.

Radelet, M. L., & Lacock, T. L. (2009). Do executions lower homicide rates? The views of leading criminologists. *The Journal of Criminal Law & Criminology, 99*, 489–508.

Severin, G. (1985, November 9). Mass murder here: Man in custody after five family members slain. *The Register-News*, p. 1-A.

Snyder, R. (1995, November 8). The Tommy Odle murders: Ten years gone. *Morning Sentinel*, pp. 1A, 3A–4A.

Staff. (1985, November 10). Area family found slain. *Southern Illinoisan*, p. A1.

Staff. (1985, November 11). Deaths. *The Register-News*, p. 2A.

Staff. (1985, November 13a). Editorial: Media blitz. *The Register-News*, p. 4A.

Staff. (1985, November 13b). Odle family buried; son faces charges. *Southern Illinoisan*, p. A2.

Staff. (1985, November 13c). Odle formally charged with five murders. *The Register-News*, p. 1A.

Staff. (1985, November 22). Odle plea heard one day early. *The Register-News*, p. 1A.

U.S. Court of Appeals Seventh Circuit. (1962). *United States of America ex rel. James Dukes, Relator-Appellant, v. Frank G. Sain, Sheriff of Cook County, Illinois, Respondent-Appellee*, 297 F.2d 799. Retrieved from http://bulk.resource.org/courts.gov/c/F2/297/297.F2d.799.13374.html

U.S. Department of Health and Human Services. (2011). Retrieved from http://www.acf.hhs.gov/programs/cb/pubs/cm00/index.html

Websdale, N. (2010). *Familicidal hearts: The emotional styles of 211 killers*. New York: Oxford University Press.

Widom, C. S. (1989). The cycle of violence. *Science, 244,* 160–166.

———. (1998). Childhood victimization: Early adversity, later psychopathology. In B. P. Dohrenwend (Ed.), *Adversity, stress, and psychopathology* (pp. 81–95). New York: Oxford University Press.

Widom, C. S., & Maxfield, M. G. (2001, February). An update on the "cycle of violence." Washington, DC: National Institute of Justice, U.S. Department of Justice.

Wikipedia. (2011a). "Charles Brooks, Jr." Retrieved from http://en.wikipedia.org/wiki/Charles_Brooks,_Jr.

———. (2011b). "Electric Chair." Retrieved from http://en.wikipedia.org/wiki/Electric_chair

———. (2011c). "*Ford v. Wainwright.*" Retrieved from http://en.wikipedia.org/wiki/Ford_v_Wainwright

———. (2011d). "*Furman v. Georgia.*" Retrieved from http://en.wikipedia.org/wiki/Furman_v._Georgia

———. (2011e). "Gary Gilmore." Retrieved from http://en.wikipedia.org/wiki/Gary_Gilmore

———. (2011f). "*Gregg v. Georgia.*" Retrieved from http://en.wikipedia.org/wiki/Gregg_v._Georgia

———. (2011g). "John Wayne Gacy." Retrieved from http://en.wikipedia.org/wiki/John_Wayne_Gacy

———. (2011h). "Lethal Injection." Retrieved from http://en.wikipedia.org/wiki/Lethal_injection

———. (2011i). "Menard Correctional Center." http://en.wikipedia.org/wiki/Menard_Correctional_Center

———. (2011j). "Mount Vernon, Illinois." Retrieved from http://en.wikipedia.org/wiki/Mount_Vernon,_Illinois

———. (2011k). "Pontiac Correctional Center." http://en.wikipedia.org/wiki/Pontiac_Correctional_Center

———. (2011l). "Richard Speck." Retrieved from http://en.wikipedia.org/wiki/Richard_Speck

———. (2011m). "Stateville Correctional Center." http://en.wikipedia.org/wiki/Stateville_Correctional_Center

Wilson, M., Daly, M., & Daniele, A. (1995). Familicide: The killing of spouse and children. *Aggressive Behavior, 21,* 275–291.

Index

Robert E. Hanlon is a board-certified clinical neuropsychologist with a specialization in forensic neuropsychology and is an associate professor of clinical psychiatry and clinical neurology at Northwestern University Feinberg School of Medicine in Chicago. He has more than twenty-five years of experience as a forensic expert, evaluating hundreds of murder defendants and death-row inmates and testifying in many murder trials. His publications include more than thirty articles and chapters in professional journals and textbooks.

Thomas V. Odle is an inmate at the Dixon Correctional Center, Illinois Department of Corrections. In 1986 at the age of nineteen, Odle was convicted of five counts of first-degree murder and sentenced to death for the mass murder of his family. Odle has spent his entire adult life in maximum-security prisons, including seventeen years on death row. In 2003 the governor of Illinois commuted Odle's death sentence to natural life.